# JEREMIAH: WITNESS UNDER PRESSURE

**Roy L. Honeycutt, Jr.**

**CONVENTION PRESS** • Nashville, Tennessee

# Contents

This book is the text for a course in the subject area Bible Study of the Church Study Course.

Target group: This book is designed for adults and is part of the Church Study Course offerings. The 1963 statement of "The Baptist Faith and Message" is the doctrinal guideline for the writer and editor.

Dewey Decimal Classification Number: 224.2
Subject Heading    O. T.    Jeremiah
Printed in the United States of America.

# 1

# The Possibilities of Renewal

## Jeremiah 1—6

If you return, O Israel, says the LORD, to me you should return.—Jeremiah 4:1

Jeremiah's world was bounded within Judah by Kings Josiah (640-609), Jehoahaz (609), Jehoiakim (609-598), Jehoachin (598), and Zedekiah (598-587). Internationally, he lived during the resurgence of the Babylonian Empire which emerged with the fall of Nineveh in 612 BC. During the latter years of his ministry, Jerusalem twice was defeated by the Babylonians, in 597 and in 586. The second defeat ended the kingdom and introduced the sixth-century Exile. Thereby, Judah was forced to reinterpret her forms of political existence, religious practices, personal faith, and corporate theology.

Living through the most significant period of revival in Old Testament history, Jeremiah fully shared the spirit of reformation which emerged during King Josiah's reign. (See 2 Kings 22:1 to 23:30.) The reformation under Josiah during the last quarter of the seventh century BC called Judah to stand before Sinai once again. There the people were to hear and to reaffirm the covenant demands for contemporary living. To overestimate the impact of the reform movement associated with the book of Deuteronomy on Judah's faith would be difficult. Jeremiah was a product and an advocate of reformation.

Often, Jeremiah has been identified as a prophet of judgment or as the weeping prophet; however, many single qualities of his life and ministry have been magnified unduly. From numerous perspectives, Jeremiah was a prophet of renewal and hope. He called the people of Judah to renew the covenant vows that they had shattered so long before. Under constant pressure, he was a courageous witness who announced God's Word to his people. In the book of Jeremiah, the threat that was prominent in the prophets falls into the background and is replaced by complaint and the puzzling nature of Israel's apostasy. Although judgment remains, the dominant feeling of the book is that people suffer and question while God yearns. Renewal and hope are twin poles which form the structure of the book of Jeremiah.

Jeremiah also is heir to the Deuteronomic priority of the Word of the Lord. (See Deut. 4:9-24.) The term "Word" appears repeatedly in Jeremiah. Not only does the book begin with the interaction of the "words of Jeremiah" and the "word of the Lord" (1:1-2), throughout the book "word" introduces major sections. Apparently, major emphases of the book are indicated by the phrase "the word that came to Jeremiah from the Lord" or a similar phrase. Each of these used the definite article "the word" and "from the Lord" (*m'eth YHWH*) and will be used in this study of Jeremiah to distinguish major structural divisions.

The first of the major collections of Jeremiah's words appears in chapters 1—6 (probably associated with Josiah's reign). (See 3:6.) These words are concerned with the possibilities of renewal. They focus on the prophet's call as the messenger of the Lord's Word (1:1-19) and the prophetic call to renewal (Jer. 2—6).

## The Lord's Word: Clue to Renewal (1:1-19)

A significant difference exists between "words" and "word." A person often uses *word* in a deeper sense than *words*. For example, Do you have any *word* from Jim? An individual even speaks of God's revelation by referring to it as *Word*. Prophets were keenly aware of the divine presence and often said: "The word of the Lord came to me." We speak of the Bible as the written Word and of Christ the living Word

So the Word is always more than just words, regardless of how crucial the spoken and printed words may be for the biblical revelation. The Word is God's dynamic, creative presence in redeeming power. The Word is stressed strongly as the central element of Jeremiah's call experience: "Now the word of the Lord came to me. . . . I have put my words in your mouth" (1:4,9). The **Word** is always *an event or an occurrence which can be described best by using the verb of being (hayah, to be).* "Word" is the subject of verbal action, and we might translate such constructions as: *The word of the Lord happened.* Although Revised Standard Version translations consistently render the construction "came" (see v. 2), the verb suggests a far more dynamic view. The Word "was" or *happened* to Jeremiah. Every coming of the Word of the Lord was an experience in history. The Word was God's dynamic presence shared through human experience.

Prophets never felt impelled to proclaim bits and pieces of their wisdom in lieu of a Word from God. Like later apostles, they knew that they were heralds of a message from beyond themselves addressed to a situation which was beyond their ability to comprehend or to resolve. The Lord's active Word continues to be the effective clue to revitalizing congregations as well as renewing individual believers.

## The Word and the World (1:1-4)

Jeremiah's lineage was traced through his father Hilkiah (v. 1) to the priests who were exiled to Anathoth near Jerusalem because they opposed Solomon as successor to David (1 Kings 2:26-27). He brought the religious heritage of priests to the prophetic office. They had been removed from office but continued to function within the shadows of Jerusalem. Jeremiah had first-hand knowledge of Judah's rich religious and theological heritage. This heritage had been sharpened when the priests were forced to rethink their function in the context of their changing circumstances. Thus to his criticism of Judah's religious practices, Jeremiah brought a dynamic faith commitment that was balanced by a sharp detachment from Jerusalem.

In such interaction of the Word with the world, Jeremiah's words became the context for the occurrence of God's Word. Someone once said that a person cannot live in a vacuum much less prophesy in one. If the Word is to happen in a prophet's life, the biblical revelation requires the context of historical events such as those associated with Jeremiah.

## The Word and the Prophet (1:5-10)

Jeremiah's life is a miniature portrait of countless lives lived with a sense of destiny and undergirded by God's providence. In all the higher callings of life, moments of self-discovery must create the consciousness of a unique mission.

The demand for Jeremiah's decision emerged early in the narrative describing his call: " 'Before I formed you in the womb I knew you, and before you were born I consecrated you' " (v. 5). Jeremiah was chosen, consecrated, and commissioned as a prophet to the nations. He discovered in God's will a purpose that transcended the boundaries of his solitary existence. In verse 5, the Lord's biography of Jeremiah's life is compressed into eleven short words in Hebrew. In him, we discover a person chosen and prepared by God. Today, as then, a demand for such a decision grows out of the Lord's gracious giving of himself, interwoven with the choice of persons for purposes that transcend their personal agenda. Of this continuing demand for a decision which grows out of people's experience with the Lord, we might say with James Russell Lowell:

> Once to every man and nation comes the moment to decide;
> In the strife of Truth with Falsehood, for the good or evil side.

The destructive power of indecision appeared in Jeremiah's reluctance to respond positively to God's call (v. 6). His hesitation was characteristic of other call narratives such as those of Gideon, Moses, and Isaiah: "Then I said, 'Ah, Lord God! Behold, I do not know how to speak, for I am only a youth' " (v. 6). The Hebrew term **youth** denotes *a young person from the age of infancy to the period of manhood, including those who have not taken the full responsibility of a given profession.* In Jeremiah's reluctance to answer the divine call, we see that the power of indecision can destroy effective leadership, the vitality of an authentic religious experience, the sensitivity of a person's spirit, and—for a time—God's purposes.

The Lord pressed Jeremiah with his duty to make a decision (vv. 7-10). An analysis of the Old Testament call narratives suggests four elements in each: the divine word of command, the person's reluctance to obey, the divine reassurance, and the assumption of responsibility.

## The Decisive Person's Destiny (1:11-19)

What is the decisive person's destiny when that individual responds positively to the Lord's call? Two features characterize the person's destiny: (1) One focuses on the individual's role. (2) The other focuses on his/her reassurance. First, a person's destiny is bound up with that individual's role as an interpreter of contemporary events in the light of God's will. In the visions of the almond tree and the boiling pot (vv. 11-12,13-16), Jeremiah was called to interpret the relationship between divine purpose and historical events. Seeing an almond tree in bloom and knowing the similarity between the Hebrew word *shaqed* (almond) and *shoqed* (watching), Jeremiah concluded that God watches over his word to perform it in history (vv. 11-12). Persons who respond affirmatively to the divine presence are not left alone to wrest the meaning of life out of nothingness. Once the Lord's Word is set in motion in history, it has an objective reality and the power of its own fulfillment. As the almond tree *(shaqed)* blossoms in the spring (v. 11), so the Lord watches *(shoqed)* over his word (v. 12).

In the second vision, a boiling pot was about to spill over which suggested that the nations of the north were about to overpower God's people (vv. 13-16). Jeremiah was to interpret the nation's impending disintegration in the light of the Lord's relationship with his people. In a time when the people longed for a message of peace, Jeremiah declared doom. Both king and common persons wanted a prophet who would speak of Jerusalem's safety, but Jeremiah declared that the city would fall. Religious leaders wanted a colleague to support established systems, but Jeremiah declared them to be morally and spiritually bankrupt and about to be handed over to their creditors. When military and political leaders wanted a prophet to affirm the status quo and to buoy the spirits of Jerusalem's defenders, Jeremiah encouraged them to surrender. The lesson is clear: In every age, times occur when prophetic persons have no good news apart from the larger perspective of history; they must interpret life as it is.

Second, a person's destiny can be affirmed by reassurance like that which Jeremiah experienced (vv. 17-19). To function at God's command is reassuring: "But you, gird up your loins; arise, and say to them everything that I command you" (v. 17). For people who are not dismayed in the face of opposition, God gives the assurance of his care. He would make his faithful prophet "a fortified city, an iron pillar, and bronze walls" (v. 18). From the beginning, God revealed the difficult nature of Jeremiah's task. At the same time, God assured Jeremiah that his protection would extend to all opposition (v. 18). Further reassurance came in the promise of ultimate victory, whatever the opposition might be (v. 19).

## The Lord's Concern: Motivation for Renewal
## (2:1 to 3:5)

Jeremiah signaled the breaking up of certain forms of expression which were characteristic of classical prophecy. Formerly argument and threat were prominent, but Jeremiah put them in the background. Seldom did he focus on judgment as it appeared in classical prophecy. Complaint was present, but it stood on its own right rather than as a prelude to a word of judgment. The prophet's speech focused on the complaint and the senseless nature of Judah's apostasy. Dominant feelings were those of complaint, suffering, dismay, and God's yearning. Because during the first phase of his ministry Jeremiah believed that the Lord had not abandoned Jerusalem, his task was to warn Jerusalem. (See 6:8.) Consequently, exhortation was used more frequently in the earlier section than anywhere else. Jerusalem was to wash her wickedness from her heart, and then she would be saved (Jer. 3:6-10).

Questions constitute the context for 2:1 to 3:5 which is bounded by clearly marked points: "The word of the Lord came to me" (2:1) and "The Lord said to me" (3:6). Within that frame twenty-four questions appear, using seven forms of the interrogative in Hebrew.

Jeremiah 2:1 to 3:5 contains evidence that points to God's loving-kindness as the motivating power for renewal. Renewal emerges in the context of loving concern, not in the legalism of prescribed actions. Although the Lord complained about Judah's apostasy and was ready to reject his people, this section portrays the Lord's suffering, dismay, and yearning. Question after question portrays the Lord's perplexity more than his anger. In such compassion and concern, renewal had its origin.

### History's Witness: Contrasting Fidelities (2:1-3)
Jeremiah contrasted Judah's apostasy to her former fidelity. Tragically, now her fidelity was only a memory, but the Lord recalled two fundamental attitudes: devotion and love (v. 2). Both words share connotations of love. The earlier, **devotion** (*chesed*), refers to *faithful love*. It is that quality of love in a

covenant which prompts devotion. Elsewhere, the word is translated in the same context as "love" and "steadfast love" (Hosea 6:4,6). The second of the words, **"love" ('ahabah)** has been interpreted to mean *election love*. It is that quality of love which led the Lord to initiate the covenant, or of a man or woman's love for the other. In those early days, the Israelites followed the Lord "in a land not sown" (v. 2). They belonged to the Lord completely. They were "holy to the Lord" (v. 3) like the firstfruits of the harvest. When the firstfruits were dedicated to the Lord, no one could eat them without violating God's holiness and incurring divine wrath. The marked contrast between the Israelites' fidelity during their honeymoon (vv. 1-3) and their later infidelity nowhere is clarified more strikingly than in Jeremiah's charge: "They were well-fed lusty stallions, each neighing for his neighbor's wife" (5:8); or, again, "Where have you not been lain with?" (3:2).

**History's Questions: Contrasting Actions (2:4-37)**

An unusual collection of questions pose God's perplexity and frustration voiced through Jeremiah. Questions seek answers, and especially rhetorical questions which point beyond themselves to motives, attitudes, logic, folly, and self-indictment. The prophet's use of the rhetorical question achieved each of these larger purposes. In marked contrast to their early loyalty to the Lord and his faithfulness to them (2:1-3), the Israelites' experience was replete with illustrations of disloyalty. All of 2:4 to 3:5 indicts God's people for their broken relationship with the Lord. Yet Jeremiah's words were more than a mere indictment, a catalog of offenses against the Lord. They spoke of illogical, irrational actions which sowed the seeds of alienation and rejection. Using the question as a basic literary form, Jeremiah indicted Judah for base disloyalty and fading affection and for senselessness in abandoning the Lord of the covenant.

*Contrasting fidelity and apostasy (vv. 5-6,8).*—Throughout this larger section (vv. 4-8), Jeremiah used three questions to contrast loyalty and alienation. First, he asked: "What wrong did your fathers find in me that they went far from me" (v. 5)? Describing God in human terms, Jeremiah portrayed God's perplexity. What did God's relationship with his children lack that caused them to go after worthlessness and to become worthless (v. 5)? Today, as grief-stricken parents often ask,

11

"What wrong did I do that my children have responded as they have?" The Lord's question was the heartbroken cry of an anguished Father who sought answers when none were given.

Furthermore, God's people received the goodness of God's provision without acknowledging his presence. "They did not say, 'Where is the Lord who brought us up from the land of Egypt?' " (v. 6). They were not concerned about his presence. Not even among the religious leaders could concern for the Lord be observed (v. 8). In his third question Jeremiah said: " 'The priests did not say, "Where is the Lord?" Those who handle the law did not know me; the rulers transgressed against me; the prophets prophesied by Baal' " (v. 8).

*Characterizing apostasy (2:9-37).*—Through the use of questions, Jeremiah indicted Judah in six characterizations of infidelity. His contention is stated clearly: " 'Therefore I still contend with you, . . . and with your children's children I will contend' " (vv. 9-10). The Lord's lawsuit (*rib*, "contend" as in a court of law) has its rationale delineated in six lines of evidence. Each begins with the word "for" (**ki'**, although **ki'im** appears in v. 22). After each use of "for," an affirmation about Judah's apostasy is followed by a question.

1. The absurdity of apostasy (vv. 10-12) was stressed by the affirmation that neither the faraway coasts of Cyprus nor Kedar had witnessed such a thing as in Judah. " 'Has a nation changed its gods, even though they are no gods?' " (v. 11). Such action in those countries would have been absurd; yet even more absurd was Judah's changing her glory for that which did not profit, a clear reference to her infidelity.

2. Apostasy was the consequence of the people's choices (vv. 13-19). The affirmation statement isolated a double evil: " 'For my people have committed two evils' " (v. 13). They forsook the real for the false or the spurious. Furthermore, they forsook the Lord and turned to false gods, " 'broken cisterns, that . . . [could] hold no water' " (v. 13). Then the questions followed: Why had Israel (Judah) become a prey (v. 14b)? Was it because Judah was a slave, " 'a homeborn servant' " (v. 14a)? That this was not the case was implied in the rhetorical question, " 'Have you not brought this upon yourself by forsaking the Lord your God' " (v. 17)? Such questions (vv. 14,17-18) are studies in cause and effect. Judah's present and deplorable condition (effect) was the consequence of choices (cause). The closing reference to apostasy clarified it as a backsliding or

turning back (*meshuboth*, a participial form of the verb **shub**, meaning *to turn*). Such infidelity constantly concerned Old Testament prophets.

3. Apostasy was irrational (vv. 20-21). Jeremiah clearly affirmed Judah's rebellion: " 'For long ago you broke your yoke and burst your bonds; and you said, "I will not serve" ' " (v. 20). His question then isolated the irrational nature of degeneration by utilizing the analogy of a choice vine. The Lord planted Judah " 'a choice vine, wholly of pure seed' " (v. 21). The reference was to the Sorek, a red grape of choice quality. If this was true of her origins, how then had she turned degenerate and become a wild vine (v. 21)? When we have considered the good beginnings assured by the Lord's providential and loving care, apostasy was irrational.

4. Apostasy was an incurable degradation (vv. 22-25). Guilt's indelible stain was reflected in Jeremiah's affirmation: "Though [If] you wash yourself with lye and use much soap, the stain of your guilt is still before me, says the Lord God" (v. 22). People can do nothing themselves to erase the staining guilt of infidelity. The question following the affirmation was designed to stifle protestations of innocence by offering evidences of degradation: " 'How can you say, "I am not defiled, I have not gone after the Baals"?' " (v. 23). To moderns, Jeremiah's answer can be offensive, for he paralleled Judah's actions with those of a young camel interlacing her tracks: " 'Look at your way in the valley' " (v. 23). Although the figure was set in the context of sexuality, the reference was to a young camel's confusion in the desert. Female camels do not anticipate biologically the time of breeding as do other animals, including the wild ass referred to later.

Pressing the sexual analogy, Jeremiah compared Judah to " 'a wild ass used to the wilderness, in her heat sniffing the wind!' " (v. 24). The last question suggested that none needed to weary himself by seeking her, for in her month they would find her (v. 24). Israel was like a wild animal in heat. Apostasy such as that created a stain which neither lye nor soap could remove. Only in God's grace and providence could a way back emerge for wayward Israel.

5. Apostasy's hypocrisy was shameful (vv. 26-28). Verses 26-27 describe the shame of apostasy, comparing it to a thief " 'shamed when caught' " (v. 26). So the people of Judah who were guilty of idolatry, who worshiped a tree or a stone, also

would be ashamed (v. 27).

Jeremiah's "for" stresses the hypocrisy of apostasy: " 'For they have turned their back to me' " (v. 27b). Although people turned their backs to the Lord, in a time of trouble they said " ' "Arise and save us!" ' " (v. 27b). The question clearly isolates the futility of false deities: " 'But where are your gods that you made for yourself? Let them arise, if they can save you, in your time of trouble' " (v. 28). A fundamental hypocrisy is present in an apostasy when people are unable to trust the same gods in crises which they trusted during better days. Turning to the Lord only in times of trouble affirms that apostasy at base is hypocritical.

6. Apostasy is frustrating (vv. 29-37). Jeremiah focused on the large number of Judah's deities: " 'For as many as your cities are your gods, O Judah' " (v. 28b). Each city worshiped the deity associated with its geographical region. A local conception of God had displaced an understanding of his presence as universal. Following this affirmation, six questions emerge in rapid succession (assuming that vv. 33 and 36 are interrogatives, despite the RSV interjections, "How!"). The questions rushing from the text suggest the prophet's state of frustration as he spoke for the Lord. Such style underscores the premise suggested earlier: Jeremiah injected a new form into prophetic literature as he moved away from the judgment oracle to emphasize the Lord's frustration and bewilderment, his intense feelings with which the Lord witnessed apostasy.

## History's Indictment: Contrasting Commitments (3:1-5)

In contrasting Judah's commitment with true devotion, Jeremiah used divorce as an analogy of apostasy (3:1), prostitution as an illustration of unfaithfulness (3:2-3), and hypocrisy as the contrast between a person's word and deed (3:4-5). Few passages more strongly indicted Judah's lack of loyalty to the Lord or used such explicit language.

1. Appealing to the Deuteronomic law which did not allow the remarriage of divorced persons (Deut. 24:4), Jeremiah ridiculed Judah's hypocritical efforts to return. He portrayed Judah as the divorced wife who abandoned the Lord for many lovers. If custom and law prohibited the woman's return to her former husband, how much less could the Lord receive back one whose shame had been published from the hilltops.

2. Essentially, Judah's apostasy was a gross form of prostitu-

tion. If Judah presumed to return to the Lord (v. 1), she should " 'lift up . . . [her] eyes to the bare heights, and see! Where . . . [had she] not been lain with?' " (v. 2). Such perversion of life and character resulted in callousness and lack of desire to change: " 'You have a harlot's brow, you refuse to be ashamed' " (v. 3). Apostasy was attended by a corruption which eroded the people's capacity for shame.

3. Shallow phrases of endearment did not substitute for real repentance. The basic contrast between the people's prayers and their actions emerged as they called: " ' "My father, thou art the friend of my youth" ' " (v. 4). Though the most intimate relationship was depicted, it was one of word not of deed, of pretense rather than reality. The insincerity of such phrases was apparent to Jeremiah who summed up their hypocrisy: " 'Behold, you have spoken, but you have done all the evil that you could' " (v. 5).

In summary, the Lord's concern for his people was a basic motivation for renewal (2:1 to 3:5). History testified to contrasting fidelities (2:1-3). History's questions contrasted Judah's fidelity to her infidelity (2:4-8) while it outlined apostasy through a series of indictments (2:9-37). History's indictment of Judah also appeared in the contrasting commitments which marked her relationship with the Lord. In every generation, genuine renewal has its source in God and in the way in which history testifies to the need for true renewal and return to the Lord.

## 3. The Lord's Alternatives: Possibility of Renewal (3:6 to 6:30)

Since history's witness indicts human response to divine love, is renewal feasible? Can persons who have responded in ways that Jeremiah described (2:1 to 3:5) return to the Lord? More significantly, will the Lord receive people who are guilty of such apostasy and infidelity? Jeremiah addressed this issue by posing alternatives: The Lord was ready to receive his people (3:6 to 4:4), and he was ready to reject them if they did not repent (4:5 to 6:30).

### The Lord Is Ready to Receive His People (3:6 to 4:4)

In calling the people to repentance (3:6-25) and in describing the nature of repentance (4:1-4), Jeremiah affirmed that the

15

Lord stands ready to receive his people.

*The prophetic call to repentance is grounded firmly in historical events (vv. 6-25).*—Especially was this so in using Israel as an example for Judah (vv. 6-10) and in the promises which were made to both nations (vv. 11-25).

First, Judah should have learned the lesson from history, for she could observe what had happened to Israel as a consequence of her faithlessness (vv. 6-10). Throughout this section is a deliberate play on the words "faithless" (*meshubah*, the same root word as "apostasy" in 2:19) and "return" (*shub*). Seeing the way in which Israel turned away from the Lord, Judah should have returned to him (vv. 7-9). "Yet for all this her false sister Judah did not return to me with her whole heart" (v. 10). The term "return" introduces the concept of repentance through the use of the Hebrew word *shub*, meaning *to return, hence to repent.* The faithless (*meshubah*) should have repented or returned (*shub*). This was history's lesson.

Second, the promise of history emerges in two assurances made to Israel and Judah: the promise of reacceptance and glory (vv. 11-18) and the promise that family ties would be renewed (vv. 19-25). The Lord's call for repentance was clear: " 'Return faithless Israel. . . . I will not look on you in anger, for I am merciful, says the Lord' " (v. 12). Specific conditions which qualify repentance and reacceptance follow the assurance that the Lord would not "be angry for ever" (v. 12). The condition that Israel " 'only acknowledge . . . [their] guilt' " was fundamental (v. 13).

Comfort for Israel emerged in the assurance that given their return to the Lord, he would gather the Exiles and return them to Zion (v. 14). The phrase "for I am your master" (v. 14) is an effective play on the word *Baal*. The Hebrew text used *ba'al* as a verb: For I am master (*ba'al*) over you. Not the Canaanite deity Baal but the Lord would be *ba'al* (master, lord) over Israel. In addition to this assurance of return and comfort in the lordship of Yahweh, which is expressed in poetic structure, a prose section appears which further describes Israel and Judah's reunion. The section also describes the nature of life restored in Jerusalem (vv. 15-18).

The Lord also promised the renewal of family ties in response to repentance (vv. 19-25). God's purposes were like the dreams of a father for wayward children (vv. 19-20). The intimacy of this hope is sketched in the portrait of God's reflecting

16

to himself on his children's action. Although the Revised Standard Version translates the verb as "thought" (v. 19), the verb in the Hebrew text more commonly is translated "said" (*amar*). That the Lord's hopes for his children proved futile is equally evident: " 'Surely, as a faithless wife leaves her husband, so have you been faithless to me' " (v. 20).

Yet Jeremiah could not leave the issue without again sketching God's promises in terms of repentance that renews God's family (vv. 21-25). He described the restored family in an idealized portrait composed of three scenes. Penitent sons were heard " 'weeping and pleading . . . because they . . . [had] perverted their way, they . . . [had] forgotten the Lord their God' " (v. 21). Such penitence would be prerequisite to being restored to God's family. We can be assured that such penitence always counter-balances a pleading father's urging his alienated children to return: " 'Return, O faithless sons, I will heal your faithlessness' " (v. 22a).

Professing children who seek the Lord and acknowledge the futility of abandoning him as their hope of salvation consummates the picture of the restored family: " 'Behold, we come to thee; for thou art the Lord our God. Truly the hills are a delusion. . . . the Lord our God is the salvation of Israel' " (vv. 22-23). As the confession continued, the Lord's children acknowledged that from their youth "the shameful thing" (v. 24) literally had eaten them—a reference to non-Israelite worship. They acknowledged their shame, their sin against the Lord, and their disobedience (v. 24). Seldom in the Bible do we discover a pattern for the renewal of the broken family expressed so clearly.

*The prophetic call to repentance clarifies the nature of authentic repentance (4:1-4).*—Real repentance is intensely personal: " 'If you return, . . . to me you should return' " (v. 1). Because sin ultimately is directed toward God, repentance can be directed only to him if it is to be authentic and to effect renewal. Such repentance has negative and positive characteristics. Negatively, God's directive was: " 'Remove your abominations from my presence, and do not waver' " (v. 1). Positively, true repentance included the affirmation of the Lord as dynamically real and effective in a person's life: " ' "If you swear, 'As the Lord lives' " ' " (v. 2), apparently referring to a phrase that Judah used in worship to affirm Yahweh's presence. This affirmation had to be accompanied by three qualities

17

of covenant life: truth, justice, and uprightness (righteousness). Following the characterization of real repentance, Jeremiah exhorted the people to implement that repentance so necessary for renewal: " 'Break up your fallow ground, and sow not among thorns' " (v. 3). Circumcision as a rite of passage into covenant life was not nearly as important as its symbolic significance for opening one's heart to the Lord: " 'Circumcise yourselves to the Lord, remove the foreskin of your hearts' " (v. 4).

In summary, the Lord's first alternative was clear: Renewal was possible on the basis of true repentance, for the Lord was ready to receive his people.

### The Lord Is Ready to Reject His People (4:5 to 6:30)

The Lord's willingness to receive his people should not obscure the possibility of rejection. Equally, he was ready to reject his people who willfully disobeyed. The pattern of choices was established and waited for Judah to make the next move. Such a decision ultimately rested with God's people, for he created them with a freedom to act. This was an inherent part of their creation in God's image. Jeremiah sketched the alternative—the return of chaos (4:5-31). He also sketched the alternatives to chaos (5:1-30) and the nature of the end should it come for God's people (6:1-30).—

The threat of chaos (4:5-31).—These oracles form part of Jeremiah's war poems (4:5 to 6:30). They focus on the threat of invasion by the Babylonians pictured in the return of chaos much like that of the creation narrative. (See 4:23.) Through six oracles, Jeremiah sketched the imminent return of chaos because the Lord's people failed to return to him.

1. Jeremiah proposed flight as the first recourse to chaos (vv. 5-8), for evil was coming from the north, like a lion from its thicket (vv. 6-7). The trumpet of alarm would be blown throughout the land; the people would assemble in fortified cities (v. 5). Yet, all of this would be to no avail (v. 8). Flight was a normal response to catastrophe; yet, Judah's dilemma would be compounded because the people would have no place to run, no hiding place.

2. Fear in the face of chaos would characterize the leaders (v. 9.)

3. The winds of chaos (the Babylonians) would smite Jerusalem. Such winds were not the gentle winds used to winnow

grain; they were hot winds from the desert (v. 11). In response to the chariots coming like a whirlwind with horses swifter than eagles (v. 13), Jeremiah again urged his people to repent (v. 14).

4. Swirling clouds of destruction which engulfed Jerusalem prompted the prophet to empathize with the people (vv. 19-22). The language is graphic and intimately personal. Speaking in pain for his people, his heart beating wildly, Jeremiah cried: " 'I cannot keep silent; for I hear the sound of the trumpet' " (v. 19). His response to the invader's devasting effects was more than sympathy, for he grieved, too: "How long must I see the standard, and hear the sound of the trumpet?" (v. 21). Until a prophet has borne the grief of his people empathetically, he has not paid the price required of those who prophesy.

5. Chaos always comes again when people live apart from God's sustaining grace (vv. 23-29). Reference to the words "waste and void" (v. 23) suggests that Jeremiah saw the possibility of the cosmos' return to the chaotic condition of "waste and void" which characterized the earth in the creation narrative. In the flood narrative, chaos came again as the waters returned to cover the earth, somewhat like the watery beginnings (Gen. 7:11-24). To Jeremiah, chaos always threatened to return.

6. Superficial embellishments are futile alternatives to the reality of chaos (vv. 30-31). The enemies' attacks in full force caused the cities' people to take flight, to climb among the rocks, and to hide in thickets (v. 29). In the context of such disintegration, Jerusalem's response was ridiculous to the point of being almost comic. Dressed in scarlet and decked in gold, Jerusalem depended on her vain beauty to bribe her attackers (v. 30). In contrast to such vanity, verse 31 sketched a dismal picture of a woman in travail and anguish.

*The alternatives to chaos (5:1-30).*—Even in the face of chaos, Jeremiah maintained the possibility that faith had the power to deliver (5:1-9). However much unbelief might frustrate God's purposes (5:10-19) and national guilt might cause chaos to return (5:20-31), God would respond to faith.

1. The power of faith to deliver was embedded in the assumption that Jerusalem, like Sodom, could be delivered on the basis of righteous living by the few. In the context of the search for a righteous person (vv. 1-6), the depth of Jerusalem's crisis appeared. The Lord commanded Jeremiah: "Run to and fro

through the streets of Jerusalem. . . . Search her squares to see if you can find a man, one who does justice and seeks truth; that I may pardon her" (v. 1). Needless to say, Jeremiah's effort was futile. Jeremiah did not believe that sufficient moral and spiritual fiber remained in Jerusalem to avert the nation's collapse. Yet, he continued to believe that responsible persons who acted with daring integrity could avert a nation's dissolution. That conviction was only one of Jeremiah's gifts to contemporary society.

2. Despite the fact that no righteous men could be found to avert the city's collapse through their leavening influence, Jeremiah was convinced that their failure did not mean that God had failed (vv. 10-19). That many people no longer believed in the reality of God's presence was obvious from some people's cynical observation: " ' "He [God] will do nothing; no evil will come upon us. . . . The prophets will become wind; the word is not in them" ' " (vv. 12-13). Yet the fulfillment of the Lord's purposes was assured through the prophet's ministry (v. 14) and in the role of nations warring against Judah (vv. 15-17). Despite the havoc of war and the alienation of many people because of unbelief, the end was not absolute: " 'I will not make a full end of you' " (v. 18).

3. National guilt was responsible for the chaos (vv. 20-31). The people's dullness which caused the national disaster was clear in the prophet's opening address: " 'O foolish and senseless people, who have eyes, but see not, who have ears, but hear not' " (v. 21). God's creative action established " 'the sand as the bound for the sea, a perpetual barrier which it cannot pass' " (v. 22), but Judah was not as responsive as the sea! They had " 'turned aside and gone away' " (v. 23). Their iniquities and their sins had kept good from them (v. 25), and they had wreaked havoc in social relationships (vv. 26-29). Even religious leaders were party to the national guilt: "The prophets prophesy falsely, and the priests rule at their direction; my people love to have it so" (v. 31). With that sombre note, Jeremiah concluded his brief attempt at suggesting an alternative to chaos (5:1-31). He soon discovered that no way was open to avert the chaos generated by the loss of God's presence. With a haunting echo, his final question has floated across the centuries to stalk people who reject the alternatives to chaos: "What will you do when the end comes?" (v. 31).

When the end comes (6:1-30).—Jeremiah was convinced that

the end had come. Not only time but God's patience had run out for a people so dull and lacking perception. What characterized the demise of the nation?

1. Jeremiah graphically described the assault on the city (vv. 1-8) as he compared Jerusalem with a well that contained wickedness: " 'As a well keeps its water fresh, so she keeps fresh her wickedness' " (v. 7).

2. Jeremiah saw the end as a time of gleaning like the grape-gatherer who stripped away the grapes (vv. 9-15). He implied the total stripping of the city: " 'Pass your hand again over its branches' " (v. 9b).

3. When the end came, people would reject the ancient ways (vv. 16-21). Jeremiah turned to an alternative to chaos and challenged the people: " 'Ask for the ancient paths, where the good way is; and walk in it, and find rest for your souls' " (v. 16). Such a path brought rest because it was a good way—the way of God's purpose. However, "They said, 'We will not walk in it' " (v. 16). To the warning blast of the watchman's trumpet they said, " 'We will not give heed' " (v. 17).

4. The end would be attended by destruction through historical processes (vv. 22-26). An enemy "from the north country" without specific identification would come in battle array against Jerusalem (vv. 22-23).

5. When the end came, the assayer would have finished his work (vv. 27-30). The pronoun "you" is singular in verse 27. It suggested that Jeremiah may have been the assayer of his people. God's people experienced fires of adversity which assayed the content of their lives: " 'The bellows blow fiercely, the lead is consumed by the fire; in vain the refining goes on, for the wicked are not removed' " (v. 29). The failure of the refining process had an obvious effect: " 'Refuse silver they are called, for the Lord has rejected them' " (v. 30).

The book of Jeremiah opens with a lengthy analysis of the possibilities of renewal (1:1 to 6:30). The Lord's Word is the clue to renewal (1:1-19) just as his concern forms its motivation (2:1 to 3:5). In any renewal effort, the Lord's alternatives are two: He is ready to receive his people (3:6 to 4:4) just as he is ready to reject them (4:5 to 6:30).

# Lessons for Life from Jeremiah 1—6

*Despite his desperate circumstances, Jeremiah's conviction that life could be transformed through God's creative presence enabled him to live victoriously.*—When a person lives in adversity, the possibilities of renewal can become a source of hope which will enable that individual to live triumphantly. So far as we know, Jeremiah never outlived his crises; he remained a witness under pressure. But he was transformed in the process. Such transformation of life despite the pressure of crises is one key to victorious living.

*The authentic revival of divine-human relationships rests in the dynamic power of God's Word which claims human lives.*—The Word interacting with the world generates the power of new relationships. Jeremiah's hope for God's people did not rest in his conviction of their internal power of self-renewal. It rested in his abiding trust in the transforming power of God's Word which interacted with people. The priority of God's Word is basic to renewal of personal and corporate relationships with God and other people.

*The need for current renewal is reflected in the character of the times.*—History affirms the priority of renewal as the focus of hope. Just as apostasy's traumatic effects became the basis for Jeremiah's call to covenant renewal, so our society's disintegrating character trumpets the call to spiritual and moral renewal.

*The alternatives of life which Jeremiah stated so forcefully, yet so simply, continue to place responsibility for today's society where it belongs.*—Persons created in God's image are decision-makers who can respond to alternatives and who are responsible for those choices. This was true of Jeremiah's generation; it is true of every era. The Lord stands ready to respond to human decisions. He is ready to receive his people just as he is ready to reject. When people in another century write this generation's history, let no one misunderstand: We will be the ones who are responsible for our situation. We alone hold the power to alter our circumstances, for God is ready to receive or to reject any given generation.

# Personal Learning Activities

1. Jeremiah is described best as (choose the correct response from the list):
   _____(1) The weeping prophet
   _____(2) The prophet of judgment
   _____(3) The prophet of renewal and hope
2. For Jeremiah, the Word was God's dynamic presence shared through human experience. True _____ False _____
3. From the following list, select the kings of Judah during whose reigns Jeremiah prophesied.
   _____(1) Ahab          _____(5) Jehoiakim
   _____(2) Josiah        _____(6) Jehoiachin
   _____(3) Jehoahaz      _____(7) Hezekiah
   _____(4) Uzziah        _____(8) Zedekiah
4. Renewal for Jeremiah's people hinged on their _____  _____ . (Select the correct response from the list.)
   (1) Offering sacrifices       (3) Repenting, returning
   (2) Obeying the Law           (4) Preparing militarily

**Answers:**
1. (3); 2. True; 3. (2), (3), (5), (6), (8); 4. (3).

# 2

# Choosing Life's Way

## Jeremiah 7—10

> The harvest is past, the summer is ended, and we are not saved.—Jeremiah 8:20

Choices and their consequences eloquently reflect people's freedom to chart their courses. God created all persons with the freedom and power of choice which included obvious risks, for God and for persons. As many parents know from experience, authentic freedom for a child means to run the risks of both success and failure. So with God, the Father, the risks of persons' freedom are run in the conviction that choices without risks actually are no choices and reflect less than authentic decision-making. People cannot avoid the risk of choices. They especially cannot avoid the most important risk—that of choosing life's way. People will adopt a guiding life-style, a basic philosophy which governs their lives. Jeremiah's concern for the renewal of Judah's relationship with the Lord presupposed that Judah should make specific choices. In assessing those choices, Jeremiah traced three stages of development: the hazards of unwise choices (7:1 to 8:3; see 26:1-24); the consequences of unwise choices (8:4 to 9:22); choosing life's way wisely (9:23 to 10:25).

## The Hazards of Unwise Choices (7:1 to 8:3)

Jeremiah's authority to counsel rested in the reality of his source in God: "the word that came to Jeremiah from the Lord"

(v. 1). Chapters 7—10 constitute an integrated section of materials. This fact is suggested by the appearance of the unique form of the divine Word in 7:1 and in 11:1, but nowhere between those junctures. This construction utilizes the definite article "the word" and "from the Lord." Apparently, the phrase "the word that came to Jeremiah from the Lord" (7:1) was a way of distinguishing major components of the book. The present study of Jeremiah follows that thesis in the structure of this book.

## Choosing a Place Rather than a Person (7:1-20)

Spoken at the Temple gates in the beginning of Jehoiakim's reign (26:1), Jeremiah's sermon accused the people of having trusted unduly in the Temple while minimizing God's revelation and demands (v. 4; see 26:1-9). No one should contend that such misplaced confidence was deliberate. Consciously, Judah had not substituted the place of worship for the Person who should stand at the center of worship. Such sublimation of God's priority in worship was an erosive process which occurred over long periods of time and often through the actions of persons with noble motivations.

*A deceived people's deceptive words are unacceptable to God (7:1-4)*.—All worship ideally contains a system of thought or theology, a pattern for expressing the joy of salvation through worship, and a system of ethics which impowers conduct. If the Temple was to continue as a place where the people of Judah might gather, Jeremiah's call to ethical living would have to be heeded: " 'Amend your ways and your doings, and I will let you dwell in this place' " (v. 3). People who trust in deceptive words are deceived if they believe that words of endearment for the religious items may be substituted for a personal experience with God. Such shallow acts on the part of worshipers at the Temple led the prophet to warn, " 'Do not trust in these deceptive words: "This is the temple of the Lord, the temple of the Lord, the temple of the Lord" ' " (v. 4).

Knowing that the Lord had delivered Jerusalem from the Assyrians a century earlier (Isa. 7:1-17), the people of Judah presumed on his continuing protection. Their logic was simple and clear. The Lord was within the Temple; the Temple was located in Jerusalem; hence, Jerusalem was safe. Unfortunately, they were not the last to move from a valid premise to a false conclusion. Not a person's place of worship, but that individu-

al's relationship with the Lord brings deliverance.

*God's demands stand in marked contrast to deceptive words (7:5-7).*—If the Temple was unable to guarantee Jerusalem's security, what could? First, the people had to change their ways (repent): " 'For if you truly amend your ways and your doings . . . then I will let you dwell in this place' " (vv. 5,7). The Hebrew grammatical construction has the effect of intensifying the action in "amend" as though to say: If you genuinely amend. "Truly" in the Revised Standard Version does not render a word for truth (*'emeth*) but is an effort to convey the idea of intensity of action. The same construction is used in urging justice: "truly execute justice" (v. 5). Renewal of life in God's presence begins with authentic response in which a person truly changes his or her ways.

Second, when people amend their ways, the change should lead to justice toward other persons (v. 5). This renewal of relationship involves social concern toward three groups that typified the helpless in Judah: "if you do not oppress the alien, the fatherless or the widow" (v. 6). The alien or stranger (*gur*) was a person who lived permanently in Judah, but who had no inherited rights. Thus, the person was liable to mistreatment as were the orphans and the widows for whom society had no structured support. Furthermore, innocent blood was not to be shed. Perhaps, "this place" (v. 6) referred to the Temple rather than to Jerusalem, and the people's devotion to the Lord was to be manifest in their refusal to "go after other gods to . . . [their] own hurt" (v. 6). Only on those conditions would the Lord assure their dwelling in the land that he gave to their fathers forever (v. 7).

*Degenerate conduct was attendant to superficial religious experiences (7:8-11).*—Two questions focused on the people's superficial dependence on the Temple. The first question contrasted immoral conduct with pious professions of dedication: " 'Will you steal, murder, commit adultery, swear falsely, burn incense to Ba'al, and go after other gods?' " (v. 9). After Jeremiah referred to five of the Ten Commandments, he asked: " 'Will you . . . then come and stand before me in this house . . . called by my name, and say, "We are delivered!" ' " (vv. 9-10)? The second question sarcastically inquired about the polarization of the purpose for the Lord's house: " 'Has this house, which is called by my name, become a den of robbers in your eyes?' " (v. 11). The Lord validated the charge as he said, " 'I myself have seen it' " (v. 11).

*Destruction of deceived persons (7:12-20).*—Because of the people's perverted religious attitudes toward the Temple (vv. 1-11), the Lord suggested that they consider what had happened to Shiloh as a result of Israel's wickedness (v. 12). Because the Lord called and no one listened and spoke but no one answered (v. 13), he would do to Jerusalem as he had done to Shiloh (vv. 14-15). That such a fate could not be averted was suggested in the Lord's command as he told Jeremiah not to pray for the people (v. 16).

Judah had shown no desire for renewal. This was validated by the question, " 'Do you not see what they are doing in the cities of Judah and in the streets of Jerusalem?' " (v. 17). Then Jeremiah described how all the people were caught up in the worship of the Babylonian Astarte, "the queen of heaven" (v. 18), a goddess. Such action did not provoke the Lord to anger so much as it provoked the people to confusion (v. 19). Apart from the radical fires of adversity which could purge away the dross of hypocrisy that had infiltrated Judah, no other hope appeared. This fate is certain for all who trust in their own creation.

## Choosing a Pattern of Worship Rather than a Presence (7:21-34)

What was true of the Temple was true of sacrifice: People did not deliberately make sacrifice superior to God's presence. Yet through constant attention to the patterns of worship, Judah lost touch with God's presence. Sadly, the means of worship became the goal of worship; people began to assume that sacrifice was an end rather than a means.

*Multiplying the forms of worship (7:21).*—God addressed a note of ridicule to the elaborate systems of worship which had been allowed to overshadow his presence: " 'Add your burnt offerings to your sacrifices, and eat the flesh' " (v. 21). Burnt offerings and sacrifices were Levitical offerings, and eating the flesh was one facet of the communion meal that added meaning to the regular sacrifices. Hence, nothing was innately wrong with the people's actions in verse 21. In order to discover Judah's offense, we must turn to motive or attitude, to the senseless increase of sacrifices beyond what was required or to other areas of attitude. Probably the people multiplied sacrifices on the assumption that a large number would please

God; but in the process, they obscured the reality of his presence. The fallacy is old. People succumb to the error of believing that they can impress God with the number of things they do as opposed to the quality of who they are.

*Motivation for worship (7:22-26).*—Verses 22-26 presuppose that the motivation and spirit which attended the sacrifice determined its effectiveness. Jeremiah probably did not try to set the time when sacrifices began (v. 22) as much as he stated a principle. Being the people of God was not preconditioned by anything other than his loving grace in choosing the Israelites. (See Deut. 7:7.) Neither law, sacrifice, nor any other action precedes individuals' unconditional response to God: " 'Obey my voice, and I will be your God, and you shall be my people' " (Jer. 7:23).

Israel saw no form at Sinai but heard a voice; through the ages, individuals' fidelity to God's Word remains the absolute criteria for assessing their relationship to him. As a highly active society, Israel multiplied its forms of worship at the price of the divine presence: " 'Yet they did not listen to me. . . . They did worse than their fathers' " (v. 26).

*Abusing sacrifice (7:27 to 8:3).*—God intended for sacrifice to be embedded in worship. Sacrifice was to be like a two-way ladder bearing traffic to and from God's presence. It lifted people's spirits to the Lord and also assured them of his presence in life. Yet they had abused sacrifice to the point that it became ineffective as well as a barrier to God's presence. Why was that true? (1) The people who would not listen to the Lord's Word through the prophet abused sacrifice. Judah's attitude of self-security generated through abuse of sacrifice contributed to the people's rejection of the Lord's Word. (See vv. 27-28.) (2) Judah corrupted sacrifice with pagan influences which led the people to construct a high place in the valley of Hinnom for sacrificing their children (vv. 29-34). Such abuse brought judgment—God's wasting the land and silencing the bride and bridegroom's mirth, gladness, and joy (v. 34). (3) When Judah abused sacrifice or worship as a whole which symbolized the nation's relationship with God, the resulting judgment was complete desecration of the land (8:1-3). Judah took extreme care for the dead. This underscores the note of condemnation in God's threat that the bones of kings, princes, priests, prophets, and people would "be spread before the sun and the moon and all the host of heaven" (vv. 1-2). God's judgment was that their bones would be desecrated and left before the symbols of the foreign deities they had worshiped: the sun, moon, and stars!

## The Consequences of Unwise Choices (8:4 to 9:22)

Always, the seriousness of choices is related to the degree of the consequences for the decision-makers and for others who are associated with them. In Jeremiah's day, if the consequences had been less severe the choices would not have been as serious for his generation. The prophet traced the results of Judah's unwise choices as they affected the decision-makers and the prophet; then, he characterized the impact of wrong choices on the total community.

### Decision-Makers' Consequences for Choices (8:4-17)

What consequences flow from unwise choices, especially when they affect a person's relationship with God? In tracing the impact of Judah's wrong choices, Jeremiah sketched—for every generation—the portrait of life with less than the full impact of God's presence.

*Abandoning the Lord is irrational (8:4-7).*—People are more rational in the common experiences of life than they are in their relationships with God. For example, Jeremiah illustrated the irrational nature of alienation: " 'When men fall, do they not rise again? If one turns away, does he not return?' " (v. 4). Obviously, the answers are yes. Jeremiah asked: " 'Why then, has this people turned away in perpetual backsliding?' " (v. 5). If they applied logic to their relationships with God, they would return to him. Yet, no one turned to the Lord; they ran " 'like a horse plunging headlong into battle' " (v. 6). Even birds that migrated, such as the " 'turtledove, swallow, and crane . . . [kept] the time of their coming' " (v. 7). Even birds that migrate reflect greater judgment, a keener sense of direction, and a better capacity for timing their return than do persons who are alienated from God.

*Rejecting the Word of the Lord is illogical (8:8-13).*—Jeremiah seemed to reflect the tensions between three classes of people in Judah: the wise, the priest, and the prophet. He accused the wise men of having rejected the Word of the Lord (v. 9) and earlier ridiculed those who said: " 'The law of the Lord is with us' " (v. 8). Even the prophets were chastened: " 'From prophet to priest every one deals falsely' " (v. 10). God through Jeremiah said: " 'They have healed the wound of my people lightly, saying, "Peace, peace," when there is no peace' " (v. 11). Although they claimed to be wise (v. 8), their actions created a shameless and sterile religious community. Even the prophets " 'were not at all ashamed; they did not know how to blush' " (v. 12). We should not be surprised that such a community also should be religiously sterile: " 'When I would gather them, says the Lord, there are no grapes on the vine, nor figs on the fig tree . . . and what I gave them has passed away from them' " (v. 13). That generation's tragedy was compounded because the people failed to produce new growth, and they could not maintain what they had been given.

*Essentially, alienation from God is self-destructive (8:14-17).*—That Judah reached the point of living without hope was reflected in the call, "Let us go into the fortified cities and perish there" (v. 14). They believed that God had doomed them to perish, and although they "looked for peace, no good came" (vv. 14-15). The sound of the invading Babylonian army was heard from as far away as Dan in the north (v. 16), and the enemy was pictured as already having come to devour " 'the land . . . the city and those who . . . [dwelt] in it' " (v. 16). Judah reaped the consequences of her unwise choices, and her destruction was a form of national suicide.

## Consequences of Choices for Persons Identified with Decision-Makers (8:18 to 9:3)

While aboard a flight into Chicago, I talked with a young man who described his "religious" posture. "I don't do anything to hurt myself or anyone else," he said as he awkwardly sought to converse with a theological professor.

What we do reaches out to touch others' lives. Those people who insist, "What I do doesn't hurt anyone else," have not recognized the nature of human existence. Concerning Judah's choices, that was true; the people reached beyond themselves to touch Jeremiah's life and to wring from him those anguished cries in chapters 8 and 9.

*The inner grief of a loving bystander (8:18-22).*—Jeremiah grieved for his people as he heard them cry throughout the land (v. 19) and question the reality of the Lord's presence in Jerusalem. Even their cry of desperation was provocative, for they presumed on God's presence as they identified him with the

Temple. Jeremiah also grieved because time had run out; no one could help them: " 'The harvest is past, the summer is ended, and we are not saved' " (v. 20). The wound of Judah became Jeremiah's wound: "For the wound of the daughter of my people is my heart wounded, . . . dismay has taken hold on me" (v. 21). Jeremiah embodied the principle that until a prophet weeps for the people, he has no basis for prophesying. His grief was deeper because the situation could have been otherwise. The response to his question, "Is there no balm in Gilead? Is there no physician there?" (v. 22), is positive. A balm was available in Gilead, just as physicians were there. This was not Judah's problem; her failure rested deep in her unwillingness to seek the physician or to apply the balm!

The impulse to flee the situation (9:1-3).—Two of Jeremiah's requests focused on the depth of his grief. First, he asked that someone fill his head with water that he might weep day and night for his people (9:1; 8:23 in the Hebrew text and perhaps to be read with chapter 8). This desire has been interpreted in a way that gives Jeremiah the proverbial name "the weeping prophet." His strength set his weeping in the larger context of a maturer identity with his people whose lives had been shattered. Second, Jeremiah used the same grammatical construction as he asked that someone give him a lodging place in the wilderness so that he might leave behind the consequences of Judah's unhappy choices. Despite long-standing opportunities, the people did not know him, said the Lord (v. 3). Does a time come when a person's best recourse is to abandon such evil people to the results of their choices?

## Consequences of Choices for the Community (9:4-22)

When choices go wrong and persons suffer the results of misplaced confidences, what happens to the community? Jeremiah described the community from three perspectives: the lack of trust which marked their common life (vv. 4-6), the hypocrisy that pervaded the community (vv. 7-9), and the final collapse of a morally corrupt community (vv. 10-22).

Distrusting one another (9:4-6).—One of sin's continuing effects is the destruction of trust in human relationships. From the beginning, doubt attended the rupture of divine-human relationships: "Did God say?" (Gen. 3:1). The caution in 9:4 was grounded in a lack of trust: "Let every one beware of his neighbor." The Hebrew text used a more graphic verbal form than the

Revised Standard Version: Let every person truly guard himself (*shamar*) from his neighbor. Jeremiah made a deliberate play on the name **Jacob** and the verb **ya'qob,** *he supplants*. Jeremiah said that they were *not to trust* **(ya'qob)** any brother, for every brother was a *supplanter* (v. 4, **ya'qob**), just as Jacob supplanted his brother Esau! People who deceived others, spoke lies, and committed iniquity (v. 5) soon accepted ruptured human relationships as normative. They became "too weary to repent" (v. 5).

*Deceiving one another* (9:7-9).—Because of the community's character, the Lord could do nothing other than to "refine them and test them" (v. 7), for judgment through warfare and exile would purge the dross from the fine metal. To justify the refining process, Jeremiah cited the people's hypocritical deceptions. An individual spoke peaceably **(shalom)** to his neighbor, but in his heart he planned an ambush (v. 8). If God should be silent when faced with such hypocrisy, he would compromise his integrity: "Shall I not punish them for these things . . .; and shall I not avenge myself?" (v. 9).

*Destroying one's self* (9:10-22).—The lack of an inner moral quality flowing out of relationships with the Lord destroyed the nation. This lack of moral quality was a form of national suicide. (See 8:14-17). Jeremiah isolated the ruin symbolized through national calamity (vv. 10-11), identified a reason for such destruction (vv. 12-16), and called for mourners to lament the deceased nation (vv. 17-22). His portrayal of a national calamity reflects overtones of the earlier picture of chaos (4:23-26).

The reason for such destruction was given: "Why is the land ruined?" (v. 12). The Lord answered, "Because they have forsaken my law . . . and have not obeyed my voice or walked in accord with . . . [my voice], but have stubbornly followed their own hearts and have gone after the Baals" (vv. 13-14). Consequently, the end had come for the nation. "Wormwood" and "poisonous water" stood in marked contrast to the provision of manna and water in the wilderness (v. 15).

Convinced that the end had come for Judah, Jeremiah called for the mourners to lament her death. First, he called for professional mourners (v. 18). Then he called on families to lament the passing of the nation's men (vv. 20-22). Only the women and the daughters were addressed on the assumption that the men had been killed (v. 21). Jeremiah noted the grave extent of such a calamity: " 'The dead bodies of men shall fall like dung upon the open field, like sheaves after the reaper, and none shall gather them' " (v. 22).

When people place their confidence somewhere other than in their relationship with God, they must face the consequences for their foolish choices. All segments of society bear the brunt of such faithlessness.

## Choosing Life's Way Wisely (9:23 to 10:25)

The oracles on the demise of the nation and the folly of their poor choices and misplaced confidences are followed by an oracle on true wisdom (vv. 23-25). That sequence is pertinent. Then life's options were contrasted (10:1-16) and the people who heard the prophet or who read his words were encouraged to choose wisely (vv. 17-25).

### Glorying in the Knowledge of God (9:23-25)

Fundamental to the prophet's presupposition was his assumption that all persons seek life marked by celebration and praise (*hll*). But inevitably they must make choices and must weigh one type of glory (*halel*) against another. The Revised Standard Version does not distinguish between the rendering of "glory" (v. 23) and other references to an entirely different Hebrew word which is translated "glory." The latter term could refer to God's glory or to a person's glory or significance.

Jeremiah used the Hebrew verb *halel* which could be translated *praise* or *celebration*. It is the same verb from which the word *hallelujah* ("praise the Lord"; *halelu*, *praise ye*; plus *yah*, an abbreviation for Yahweh or Lord) comes. Hence, it was not glory in the sense of exaltation which occupied Jeremiah's attention, but celebration or praise.

What is the source of celebration for a person's life? Three primary categories of human achievement emerge as central to the quest for celebration and praise: Wisdom, might, and wealth (v. 23). Yet an individual will not choose life's way wisely if these become the pillars on which that person celebrates life. They cannot sustain the celebration in life.

People who choose life's way wisely will heed Jeremiah's counsel: " 'Let him who glories glory in this, that he understands and knows me, that I am the Lord who practice steadfast love, justice, and righteousness' " (v. 24). The Lord remains the reason for the celebrative life. To understand and know him sets parameters for a person's life as he/she lives the life of praise and celebration (**halel**). Yet to know God implies that an individual understands those recurring words of covenant life: kindness (*chesed,* or *faithful love*), *justice,* and *righteousness.* Earlier, Jeremiah called for comparable qualities in the people's lives: truth, justice, uprightness (4:2). When a person experiences ("knows," v. 24) the Lord, his or her life is characterized by faithful love, justice, righteousness, and truth.

## Contrasting Life's Options (10:1-16)

Central to the renewal effort under Josiah was the challenge for Judah to stand again before Sinai and hear God's Word. Such an experience embodied obvious choices and appears throughout the book of Deuteronomy. Nowhere does it appear more pointedly than in the polarities of good and evil, life and death: "See, I have set before you this day life and good, death and evil" (Deut. 30:15). Such choices confront every generation. In that context, Jeremiah challenged Judah with the options of lifeless idols or a living God.

*Lifeless idols (10:1-5).*—Jeremiah's debate on idolatry utilized ridicule and irony. He sought to reduce to absurdity the position of any people who might support such pagan imitations. Judging the customs of others as "false," he described a tree cut from the forest and shaped by a craftsman (v. 3). He described idols as "scarecrows in a cucumber field" (v. 5), but his most serious accusations emerged in his double charge of speech and action. Idols cannot speak a revelatory Word. They cannot act for themselves, for they cannot walk; they must be fastened with hammer and nails lest they topple over (vv. 4-5). Such inactivity stood in marked contrast with the Lord who, like a mighty warrior, again and again had entered into historical encounter with those who stood against his people. Using "good" and "evil" to describe "everything," Jeremiah summed up his attack by counseling Judah: " 'Be not afraid of them' " (v. 5). Doubtless, in today's society, many people believe that of all the Ten Commandments, a person is less likely to practice idolatry than to violate any of the other Commandments. However, the Commandment essentially prohibits reliance on rigid, static aspects of revelation as opposed to the dynamic power of the creative Word (Deut. 4:9-18). Thus, more people probably violate the Second Commandment than some people might suppose.

*The living God (10:6-16).*—After ridiculing the idols, Jeremiah carefully stated the incomparable nature of the Lord: "There is none like thee, O Lord" (v. 6). He developed the theme through three stages. (1) The Lord was incomparable because he was a living God who stood in marked contrast to idols (vv. 6-9). (2) The Lord was King: "Who would not fear thee, O King of the nations?" (v. 7). (3) Creation testifies to God's incomparable nature: "It is he who made the earth by his power" (v. 12; see vv. 11-16). The living God, King of the nations and Creator of the universe, cannot be compared with anything people know.

## Choosing Wisely (10:17-25)

If people are to choose wisely in determining their ways of life, careful attention should be given to two factors.

*Forsaking the Lord brings ruin (10:17-22).*—The ruin which attended the nation's collapse and with it the majority's hope for Judah was sketched in three portraits. Those going into Exile, with their bundles of belongings on the ground, would be slung out of the land (vv. 17-18). Jerusalem was personified as a mother whose "tent" or family would be destroyed, leaving her alone in the land with none to spread the tent (v. 20) because of the "stupid" shepherds (political leaders, v. 21). The rumor and then the reality emerged; the enemy came out of the north country to make the cities of Judah desolate (v. 22).

*Pleading for true knowledge (10:23-25).*—Effective decision-making in every area of life depends on accurate information in order for a person to choose appropriately between various options. So in 10:25, Jeremiah sought true knowledge of himself (v. 23). He sought correction of his ways at God's hand (v. 24). The prophet asked that the Lord act in history with justice that was appropriate to the unjust forces of history (v. 25). Jeremiah's perception of human nature taught him that "the way of man is not in himself" (v. 23). The Hebrew text is compressed but graphic: I know O Lord that his way (is) not for man (*'adam,* the generic word for *man* or *mankind*). Jeremiah understood that true self-knowledge flows from God who enables persons to understand themselves. Not only so, Jeremiah also understood that "it is not in man who walks to direct his steps" (10:23b).

Jeremiah also sought correction from the Lord (v. 24). If people do not know their way and cannot direct their steps, they need God's corrective action. The phrase "in just measure" could be translated *with justice* (v. 24). Jeremiah lived with openness to God's justice. He sought to avoid God's anger: "Correct me . . . ; not in thy anger, lest thou bring me to nothing" (v. 24). Wrath tempered with love, and justice without tempering, is God's promise for people who live with openness to him.

Jeremiah depended on the Lord to act in history against those nations that had devoured Jacob. Apparently, such a prayer was offered on behalf of the Northern Kingdom, for "Jacob" often refers to Israel. Jeremiah faced the future with the plea that God would act justly in history.

## Lessons for Life from Jeremiah 7—10

*Familiarity with the holy coupled with an overattention to the externals of worship may cloud a generation's understanding of God's demands.*—Like Jeremiah's era, the history of people who worship is replete with illustrations of those who exalted places and systems of worship so that they distorted God's impact on human life. Jeremiah affirmed the central role of the Temple as the place of worship and structured forms as a means to worship. However, he affirmed for successors in the covenant community the binding of worship with moral action. Only as the forms of worship are linked to the reality of life-changing relationships with God may one claim the continuing power of God's presence.

*The consequences of relying on the externals of worship rather than on the Lord are manifest in a community which is devoid of trust and morally corrupt.*—Apart from the leavening power of divine relationships, society seeks in vain for personal and national renewal. Yet too often, modern people no longer even focus on the systems of worship, however superficial such systems may have become. The basic issue for this generation is the question of the continuing reality of God. The ultimate question is not what life would be like apart from systems of worship but what society is to be like should it exclude God.

*In a society obsessed with technology and fascinated by material things, a person does well to hear in current accents Jeremiah's celebrating life through knowing God.*—To the person who seeks celebration (glory), the prophetic word is clear.

To the wise who glory in wisdom, to the mighty who glory in might, or to the rich who glory in wealth, the word is the same: " 'Let him who glories glory in this, that he understands and knows me' " (Jer. 9:24).

# Personal Learning Activities

1. Jeremiah accused his people of replacing trust in God with trust in two other things. From the following list, choose the two objects of false trust.

_____(1) The Law          _____(3) A pattern of wor-
                                          ship
_____(2) The Temple       _____(4) The ark of the cov-
                                          enant

2. Jeremiah saw clearly that acceptable sacrifice depended on (choose the correct response from the list):

_____(1) Perfect sacrifices _____(3) Motivation or spirit
_____(2) Number of sac-     _____(4) Frequency of sac-
        rifices                        rifices

3. Jeremiah's response to his people's impending judgment was _____ . (Choose the proper response from the list.)

(1) Glee                    (3) Grief
(2) Indifference            (4) Anger

4. Judah's problem was that no balm and no physician were available for the nation's healing. True _____ False _____

5. Through Jeremiah, God cautioned his people to glory in (select the correct answer from the list):

_____(1) Wisdom _____(3) Might _____(5) Wealth
_____(2) Religion _____(4) God _____(6) Health

Answers: 1. (2), (3); 2. (3); 3. (3); 4. False; 5. (4).

# 3

# Exercising One's Freedom

## Jeremiah 11—13

Can the Ethiopian change his skin or the leopard his spots?—
Jeremiah 13:23

Freedom is a gift to be exercised if it is to maintain dynamic
reality in decision-making circumstances. I have the continuing conviction that choices are not made once and settled for all
time; they are ongoing experiences. The risks of freedom are
genuine. The greater risk is not the possibility of a person's
making an improper choice but of that individual's refusing to
exercise freedom.

In calling Judah to renewal, Jeremiah presupposed the freedom of both nations and individuals to respond. Although he
dealt realistically with the bondage of people's wills at one
point, his larger perspective was their exercise of freedom. For
every person, ancient and modern, the appropriate exercise of
freedom was and is an opportunity and a responsibility.

Jeremiah called Judah to a moment of truth in exercising her
freedom. Chapters 11—13 in the book of Jeremiah focus on
hearing the Lord's call to covenant fidelity (11:1-17), conspir-
ing against the Lord's messenger (11:18 to 12:17), refusing to
obey the Lord's words (13:1-14), and testifying to pride and
human nature (13:15-27).

## Hearing the Lord's Call to Covenant Fidelity
## (11:1-17)

Central to Josiah's reform was the discovery of the Law during the renovation of the Temple. (See 2 Kings 22:8-10.) Generally, this has been associated with the book of Deuteronomy and the era of Josiah; however, the succeeding generation was affected greatly by Deuteronomic influences. The covenant was central to those influences as the clue to community for the Lord's people. Symbolically, Judah was called to stand before Sinai and to hear as Israel of old had heard the covenant life's demands. Jeremiah fully supported the reaffirmation of the covenant. (See 11:1-13.) In seeking to effect Judah's renewal, he challenged the people to respond, in freedom, to the call issued for covenant fidelity. Through his preaching in the cities of Judah (v. 6), people were forced to exercise freedom of choice in hearing the Lord's call to covenant living.

### The Contingencies of Faith (11:1-5)

Obedience to covenant demands was a primary requirement for the fulfillment of God's promise to the patriarchs. It was reflected in Jeremiah's use of the conditional clause: "That (lema'an) I may perform the oath which I swore" (v. 5). Jeremiah referred to the covenant made at Sinai. Observing the covenant was the condition for Israel's possessing Canaan. Jeremiah's dual purpose of reaffirming the Exodus covenant while at the same time encouraging the renewal of life was associated with Josiah's covenant renewal.

Jeremiah isolated four reasons for keeping the covenant:

First, he believed that the covenant shaped the form of community with God. It was the primary clue to Judah's existence as God's people, and Jeremiah identified his challenge to covenant fidelity with "the word that came . . . from the Lord" (v. 1).

Second, Jeremiah reflected the curse motif of Deuteronomy, especially the statement of curses at Mount Ebal where a twelve-curse ritual stated essential characteristics of covenant life. (See Deut. 27:15-26.)

Third, Jeremiah urged the people to keep the covenant because of the conditional nature of their relationship with God. This was not to imply that the initiating relationship with God depended on keeping the Law or the demands of the covenant, for covenant preceded Law in the Old Testament. Rather, it meant that the covenant carried stipulations for conduct. The fulfillment of God's purposes for his people was conditioned by their response.

Fourth, Jeremiah encouraged the people to keep the covenant because of the consequences of covenant keeping: "that I [God] may perform the oath which I swore . . . to give them a land flowing with milk and honey" (v. 5). Although symbols which were used to describe God's blessings varied from one generation and one culture to another, their reality remained. Persons living in relationship with the Lord had an inherent blessing. Such benefits of those relationships were by-products, however, for the primary focus of covenant life was a person's relationship with God for the sheer reality of who God is.

## The Consequences of Faithlessness (11:6-8)

Jeremiah pursued a mission through the streets of Jerusalem and the cities of Judah. He cautioned the people by reminding them of God's demand for obedience to the covenant (v. 6). The same God who gave them the land also would fulfill his threat to cast them out of the land if they were faithless. Apart from the commitment to warn the people, Jeremiah's purpose was to place his preaching in the context of earlier proclamations. His threats were not without precedent: "For I solemnly warned your fathers when I brought them up out of the land of Egypt" (v. 7). Also, the Northern Kingdom's fate should have served as a constant warning to Judah. Events taking place in Judah had occurred over a hundred years earlier in the Northern Kingdom.

## The Curse of Covenant Breaking (11:9-13)

If "curse" seems to be too strong a denunciation for covenant breaking, remember that this was Jeremiah's word from God: "Cursed be the man who does not heed the words of this covenant" (v. 3). The people of Judah, like their forefathers, had fallen away from the Lord and had conspired to violate the covenant by idolatry. Such covenant breaking constituted a revolt (v. 9a), a refusal to hear the Lord's words (v. 10a), and a commitment to other gods (v. 10b). Because of that infidelity, inescapable evil would fall upon them.

## The Consequences of a Broken Covenant (11:14-17)

People who break covenant relationships with the Lord should expect alienation from him; they have no recourse left in life's crises. Against the background of prayer in the biblical faith, the following words seem strangely out of place: "Do not pray for this people" (v. 14). Since the total biblical revelation encourages believers to pray as a proper response to God and to other persons, how can the prohibition of prayer in the book of Jeremiah be understood? (See 14:11; 15:1-9.) When people break their covenant with the Lord and deny him in better days, what right do they have to call on him in the midst of trouble (v. 14)? The timing of prayer is one factor that calls it into question. Also, in order for prayer to be effective, it must be matched by the committed lives of the people for whom prayer is offered as well as the one who prays (v. 14b). In Judah's case, the people's conduct had caused judgment which prayer could not avert.

Times come when the fruit of one's rebellion must be borne regardless of prayer. Jeremiah assumed that a person cannot pray others into a right relationship with the Lord. They must do this for themselves. Also, the loving grace of God the Father often can be expressed best through redemptive judgment rather than a soft indulgence which removes the consequences of sin, even because of prayer. Wise believers will continue to pray for others as for themselves and will let God decide whether or not their prayers are appropriate. Yet, the Lord's word that came through Jeremiah continues to emphasize that some persons and situations have gone beyond the bounds of intercessory prayer.

Not only was prayer prohibited (v. 14), but participation in the Temple services was precluded: " 'What right has my beloved in my house?' " (v. 15). Furthermore, the pronouncement of evil on such persons was symbolized graphically (vv. 16-17). Although Israel had been " 'a green olive tree' " (v. 16), the Lord would set it afire (v. 16).

## Conspiring Against the Lord's Messenger
### (11:18 to 12:17)

Proclamation like Jeremiah's seldom if ever comes without great price, and those who follow the prophetic model should be prepared for a prophet's fate. Jeremiah's Temple sermon incensed those who heard (see 7:1 to 8:3; 26:7-24); those who listened to him speak so forthrightly on covenant fidelity were incensed no less. This was reflected clearly in the conspiracy against the prophet (11:18-23) which should be examined in

42

the context of the prophet's complaint against the Lord (12:1-4), the prophet's consolation (12:5-13), and the conclusion of the conspiracy (12:14-17).

### Conspiracy Against Jeremiah (11:18-23)

Jeremiah's confidence in the people emerges in the fact that he suspected nothing at all: "The Lord made it known to me and I knew" (v. 18). "I was like a gentle lamb led to the slaughter. I did not know" (v. 19). Some people may think that Jeremiah and his trusting successors were naive and unwise in the practical affairs of human conflict. Yet, better than a cynic who refuses to trust anyone is the trusting person who is taken advantage of occasionally by scheming opponents.

How should a person respond to conspiracy such as Jeremiah faced? Neither time nor circumstance has improved on the quality of his response to opposition. He committed his cause to the Lord (vv. 20-23). People can commit a complaint or lawsuit (*rib*) to the Lord. They do this in the confidence that God judges righteously (v. 20), reveals the true nature of individuals' hearts (v. 20), restores the prophet by adopting his cause (v. 21), and comes in retribution on those who commit sacrilege against God's cause (vv. 22-23).

### Complaint Against the Lord (12:1-4)

The prosperity of the wicked was a continuing problem for the faith of Israel, especially when it was examined in the context of God's justice. (Compare Pss. 37; 73; Hab. 1:1-17.) True to human nature, Jeremiah first responded to his crisis by accusing the Lord: "Why does the way of the wicked prosper?" (v. 1). Yet in taking his cause to the Lord, the prophet disposed of it properly. A major dimension of his problem grew out of the Old Testament patterns of thought that seldom dealt with secondary causes and assumed that the Lord was responsible for everything: "Thou plantest them" (v. 2). In contrast to the wicked, Jeremiah's integrity intensified his problem (v. 3) and led him to pray that the Lord would execute judgment on those who had the Lord "near in their mouth and far from their heart" (vv. 2-4).

### Consolation for a Discouraged Prophet (12:5-13)

Someone once suggested that the Lord sought to cheer Jeremiah up by declaring that the worst was yet to come! In fact, the text *does* offer encouragement on the assumption that present trials were only forerunners of still greater heartaches (vv. 5-6). If Jeremiah was unable to bear his immediate crises, how could he survive when they were intensified: " 'If you have raced with men on foot, and they have wearied you, how will you compete with horses?' " (v. 5). The intensity of Jeremiah's trials was underscored graphically by their family dimension: "Your brothers and the house of your father, even they have dealt treacherously with you; . . . believe them not' " (v. 6).

Although the Lord's response may have been more disturbing than consoling, Jeremiah genuinely loved his people; the Lord comforted Jeremiah by indicating that he (God) had abandoned the conspirators (vv. 7-13). Yet this was the burden of Jeremiah's request (vv. 3-4) and the inevitable consequence for abandoning the covenant. The judgment came, as so often it does, in like kind. Those who had abandoned the Lord discovered that he had abandoned them: " 'I have forsaken my house, I have abandoned my heritage' " (v. 7). Jeremiah's statement that the Lord hated his people (v. 8) should be set in the context of the broader usage of the word **sane'**, for in some instances it suggests the preference of one over another. In such a context, a person might question whether the wicked actually do prosper, if in the process they lose God's presence. The Lord's heritage had become "like a speckled bird of prey," so distinct from others as to become a victim of their assaults (vv. 9-12). Because of the Lord's fierce anger, the wicked would "profit nothing. They . . . [would] be ashamed" (v. 13).

## Conclusion of the Conspiracy (12:14-17)

The prose style and fundamental theology of verses 14-17 distinguish that passage from the poetry in verses 1-13. Verses 14-17 reflect the Deuteronomic concern for repentance and renewal following judgment (Deut. 4:27-31) which also appears earlier in Jeremiah 3. Jeremiah addressed not only Judah (v. 14) but those he called "my evil neighbors who touch the heritage which I have given my people Israel to inherit" (v. 14). Although a person might be inclined to identify the "evil neighbors" as Israel of the Northern Kingdom, later references suggest a more universal perspective (vv. 16-17). Although the issue had an ambiguous element, Jeremiah seems to have addressed others around Judah who also were carried into Exile and who would experience with God's people the manifestation of his grace. Of all nations, Judah included, the Lord's last word was one of compassion and renewal for those who positively responded to him. In all generations, for those who are open to God, his last words are *grace* and *love*.

# Refusing to Obey the Lord's Words (13:1-14)

As chapter 36 makes clear, Jeremiah's words were written when they were dictated to Baruch approximately twenty years following the beginning of his prophetic ministry. No indication is given in that chapter concerning the order in which the prophetic statements were reproduced. But the book suggests, by virtue of content, that the prophetic statements were given along the lines of thematic structure rather than chronological order. Because of this, the arrangement of the book is more significant. As in the case of 13:1-14, why were the verses placed after chapter 12 rather than at some other juncture of the book of Jeremiah? Obviously, the message in chapter 13 uniquely suited Jeremiah's complaints and God's answer in the preceding chapter. Appropriately, the sign of the linen waistcloth (13:1-14) was used to emphasize the alienating power of pride (vv. 1-11) and the loss of compassion that such pride manifested (vv. 12-14).

## Pride's Alienating Power (13:1-11)

Jeremiah emphasized pride's corrupting and alienating power (vv. 1-11). Reference to "Thus said the Lord" (v. 1) and "The word of the Lord came to me a second time" (v. 3) should be placed in the context of the phrase, "The word that came to Jeremiah from the Lord" (11:1). The last phrase does not occur again until 14:1. Prophets not only conveyed God's message through words but also through symbolic acts. Hence, Jeremiah's action in buying a linen waistcloth and wearing it to communicate divine truth through prophetic symbolism was an act which people would have recognized.

Whether Jeremiah actually carried the linen waistcloth to the Euphrates long has been debated. Several interpretations have been offered: (1) He did make such a trip, actually two trips (vv. 3-7). (2) The experience was visionary, not an uncommon means of receiving divine revelation. (3) Jeremiah spoke of the journey in a literary form only; actually, he did not make two trips to the Euphrates. The basic message is the same regardless of whether or not Jeremiah made the trips. The linen waistcloth which once clung to Jeremiah (v. 2) was "spoiled" (perhaps rotten) by exposure to the Euphrates and "was good for nothing" (v. 7).

The interpretation of the symbolic action was given through the "word of the Lord" (v. 8). Two elements are integral to the meaning of Jeremiah's action. The first one focuses on the spoiling of Judah: " 'Even so will I spoil the pride of Judah . . . who refuse to hear my words" (vv. 9-10). Pride was the primary cause for that spoiling; the people's pride was basic in their refusal to hear the Lord's words and to follow them sincerely. Also, pride was basic in their commitment to follow other gods (v. 10).

From the beginning of time, pride has rested at the heart of humanity's sin. Whatever the dimension of pride's nature—whether intellectual, moral, technological, or religious—pride ruptures people's relationships with God.

The second element is that the sign of the waistcloth symbolized the close relationship which Judah once had with the Lord: " 'For as the waistcloth clings to the loins of a man, so I made the whole house of Israel and the whole house of Judah cling to me' " (v. 11). Yet even the closest relationships can be severed by the cutting edge of pride.

## Pride and the Loss of Compassion (13:12-14)

As the sign of the waistcloth indicates, pride alienates people from the Lord and signals their loss of compassion. Here as later (Jer. 25:15-29), Jeremiah used drunkenness to symbolize lack of reason, loss of good sense, and confusion. He began with a common point of agreement in his parable of the wine jar. No one could disagree with his statement that every jar would be filled with wine. If wine jars were filled with wine, then, as Jeremiah shifted his direction of argument, " 'Thus says the Lord: Behold, I will fill with drunkenness all the inhabitants of this land' " (v. 13). The climax of Jeremiah's proclamation followed: " ' "I will not pity or spare or have compassion" ' " (v. 14). Jeremiah would not say that these qualities do not exist in the Lord's relationship with his people. Rather, he intended to show that even with his children, God—the Father—reaches the point that such pity is not the appropriate response to his children's need(s).

Parental responsibility includes insisting that, in given circumstances, events and their conclusions must be experienced without sparing the child their impact. This was true for Judah and Israel. To eliminate pity and compassion for them meant the possibility of their growing in maturity which later would lead them to respond properly to the Lord.

## Testifying to Pride and Human Nature (13:15-27)

Their common focus on pride binds the prose section of verses 1-14 with the poetry of verses 15-27. (Compare vv. 8,15.) Fundamental to verses 15-27 is the contrast of judgment (vv. 15-17) and freedom (vv. 18-27). As members of the covenant community exercised their freedom, to what extent were they genuinely free? Did they have a bondage of the will that preconditioned the nature of their response to the Lord: " 'Can the Ethiopian change his skin or the leopard his spots?' " (v. 23)? If people are not genuinely free, then we may question their being able to make choices. Individuals must be free to say Yes and No.

### Pride and the Alternatives to Judgment (13:15-17)

Overwhelmed by the message of judgment, the prophet again pleaded with the people to avert mindless behavior which had caused them to act like drunken persons (vv. 12-14). Only one alternative to the nation's disintegration remained: authentic renewal of relationship with the Lord. Repentance alone would have been sufficient; however, if it were to be effective, it would have to embody three actions: (1) Listen to God, "Hear and give ear" (v. 15a). (2) Forget pride, "Be not proud" (v. 15b). (3) "Give glory to the Lord" (v. 16). The ground for renewing authentic relationships with the Lord would be real repentance—immediately!

The word before uniquely characterized Jeremiah's exhortation. Give glory to God, he said, "before he brings darkness" (v. 16). The road that Judah traveled was a dangerous one, much like a pass over steep mountains where, even in broad daylight, danger always was present. Jeremiah implored: Take the Lord as your guide and protector lest he withdraw his light, envelope you in darkness, and cause you to stumble in the lengthening shadows of dusky twilight. Jeremiah encouraged Judah to act before the people's feet stumbled on the twilight mountains, and before they looked for light and found that God had turned it into gloom and made it deep darkness (v. 16).

Should individuals reject the Lord's option of renewal and subsequent restoration, what then? Hear with one ear tuned to today's life: "But if you will not listen, my soul will weep in secret for your pride" (v. 17). Jeremiah was a brokenhearted prophet; he could do no more than weep for his people. Heartache and sorrow always accompany the loss of loved ones. Such compassion is like the Lord's when he responded to the loss of Israel with emotion and feeling: "My heart recoils within me, my compassion grows warm and tender" (Hos. 11:8). For all persons—pastors, teachers, counselors, friends, parents—often the sad recognition comes that no more needs to be said, for no counsel seems to be effective. Some persons' pride dictates a course of rebellion against those who love them most. At those times, these haunting words are for them: "My soul will weep in secret for your pride" (v. 17). Those times come when all the notes on the keyboard of one's emotions have been played. Then only the note of inexpressible sorrow remains.

### Alienation and the Bondage of the Will (13:18-27)

Despite the options posed for Judah, Jeremiah was convinced that no renewal could take place under the prevailing circumstances. Not until the people of Judah experienced the reality of the Lord's absence would they begin to treasure his presence that they had rejected. Jeremiah confronted every reader with the futility of Judah's alternatives apart from their will to respond (vv. 18-19) and the bondage of their will with its consequences (vv. 20-27).

*The futility of alternatives without will to respond (13:18-19).*—After Jeremiah gave an alternative to collapse, he assumed that Judah would not respond. Without the will to respond positively, to offer options would be futile. Only Judah could will to respond, but the people's will was frozen into inactivity. Because of this inactivity, Jeremiah called on the king and the queen mother to assume a posture of humiliation (v. 18). The southern cities were besieged or "shut up" (v. 19), and all Judah had been taken into exile (v. 19b).

*Alienation and the bondage of the will (13:20-27).*—Because Judah had rejected God's options and had no will to respond, Jeremiah asked: "Where is the flock that was given you?" (v.

48

20). Suffering like the " 'pangs ... of a woman in travail' " would seize the nation, and those whom the people of Judah had taught to be friends to them would serve as head over Judah (v. 21). Equally, the question and the answer proposed by the prophet were direct: " ' "Why have these things come upon me?" ' " (v. 22). " 'It is for the greatness of your iniquity that your skirts are lifted up' " (v. 22), a vivid picture of Judah/Jerusalem ravished by invading aliens.

Clearly Jeremiah assumed that since the people had grown accustomed to doing evil, they no more could do good than a leopard could change his spots. Only the shattering impact of national disaster and the trauma of exile could give to Judah a new perspective which would enable them to respond positively to the Lord. Often, the prophets assumed a basic disposition which precluded a return to the Lord.

We should remember that although the Lord may give persons and nations up to their evil choices (compare Rom. 1:24-27), he never gives up on them. The prophets' mission and continuing exhortations to repentance presuppose that the people were free to exercise their will. However, pessimistic passages such as verse 23 are the passing observations of a prophet made at a particular juncture in the nation's pilgrimage. They are not final statements on the nature of human freedom.

Sometimes when confronted with a moment of decision, people sin; however, they do not sin in some mechanistic way over which they have no control. In Jeremiah's generation, people believed that they were not responsible for conditions of their time. They thought that they were victims of their fathers' sins. (Compare Jer. 31:29-30.) Jeremiah spoke against such an understanding of corporate responsibility which denied that an individual would answer for himself/herself. He said that the days were coming when the children no longer would say: " 'The fathers have eaten sour grapes, and the children's teeth are set on edge' " (31:29). Rather, individual responsibility would be emphasized (v. 30).

Inherited guilt was not part of the prophetic understanding of original sin or of corporate accountability. With clear insight, the prophets understood and proclaimed that the people had the freedom to say Yes or No to God.

Perhaps the closing words of Jeremiah 13:23 clarify the nature of Jeremiah's observation: "Then also you can do good who are accustomed to do evil." People become so accustomed to a particular way of life that they are bound by that life. In this sense, people may affirm in truth that they no more can change their ways than they can change the color of their skin, or the leopard can change his spots (v. 23).

The results of sin's bondage quickly emerge in verses 24-27. Judah would be driven like chaff by a wind from the desert (v. 24). The reason for such rejection was that they had forgotten the Lord and trusted in lies (v. 25). Such an indictment suggests far more than "forgotten," such as in a lapse of memory. Rather, the word suggests an act of apostasy. Judah was humiliated in her shame, with skirts lifted up over her face (v. 26).

## Lessons for Life from Jeremiah 11—13

*Prophetic religion embodied in Jeremiah affirmed freedom as a prerequisite to a dynamic religious experience.*—Such freedom embraces the totality of human response and encompasses both the yes and the no. Persons are free to respond affirmatively to God's creative presence just as they equally are free to reject such relationship with him.

*Freedom is bounded consistently by accountability.*—The prophet's words remind every person that individuals inevitably are accountable for exercising freedom and especially for abusing it. Such accountability for the use of freedom is not only a matter of speculation for some future judgment. Rather, accountability and the effects of an individual's use of freedom constantly shape the whole person's life. In family circles, as in professional relationships or in a person's whole community, the manner in which he or she uses freedom is constantly a shaping power. The use of freedom determines the form and character of relationships. Such use of freedom is no less at work in the determination of one's personality and the character of one's life.

*The interplay of freedom and accountability underscores the contingencies of faith.*—Not only Jeremiah but the whole biblical revelation affirms that the fulfillment of God's promises is contingent on human response. Hence in Jeremiah's preaching of the covenant, emphases emerged on the demands of covenant living. The basic limitation to God's presence and blessing rests in the quality of human response. This is not to suggest that either divine presence or divine blessing is the result of human activity alone. Yet people must recognize that the willing and obedient spirit is a prerequisite to those relationships with God which are treasured most for human existence.

*Opposition to their understanding of God's will challenges persons to have a faith that is adequate for them to commit their cause to God.*—Jeremiah was not the last believer to have his understanding of God's will and his motivation in relating to others questioned. Members of his own home questioned his positions and sought his life. Confronted by such pressure, Jeremiah's temptation was to retaliate. Yet under such duress, one should hear the prophetic model for facing opposition: "To thee have I committed my cause" (Jer. 11:20).

# Personal Learning Activities

1. In his preaching, Jeremiah challenged his people to respond to the call for (choose the correct answer from the list):
   _____(1) Military pre-       _____(3) A new king
             paredness
   _____(2) Covenant            _____(4) National mourning
             fidelity
2. From the following list, select the people's response to Jeremiah's Temple sermon in 7:1-15.
   _____(1) Anger and          _____(3) Repentance
             conspiracy
   _____(2) Acceptance         _____(4) Indifference
3. Under pressures and threats, Jeremiah (select the proper responses from the list):
   _____(1) Qualified his strong words
   _____(2) Committed his cause to God
   _____(3) Resigned as a prophet
   _____(4) Voiced his complaint to God
4. According to Roy Honeycutt, in all generations, for those who are open to God, his last words are (choose the correct responses from the list):
   _____(1) Justice       _____(3) Approval
   _____(2) Grace         _____(4) Love

Answers:
1. (2); 2. (1); 3. (2), (4); 4. (2), (4).

# 4

# When All Else Fails

## Jeremiah 14—17

Though our iniquities testify against us, act, O Lord, for thy
name's sake.—Jeremiah 14:7

Clearly Jeremiah failed in his efforts to generate the desired
renewal of relationship between the Lord and Judah. Time after
time, he spoke of the possibilities of renewal (Jer. 1—6), challenged Judah to choose life's way wisely (Jer. 7—10), and urged
the proper exercise of human freedom (Jer. 11—13). Yet in the
prophet's mind, renewal remained a diminishing ideal; for the
people, it expired. With the passing years, that no renewal of
life would occur for Judah became apparent. No renewal could
take place apart from a devastation of such magnitude as to
quench the national fires and to exhaust a beleaguered people's
resources. What do people do when all else fails: prayer (14:1 to
15:9), the prophet (15:10-21), and the people (16:1-18)?
Jeremiah's hope for the future as well as his sustaining power
for his ministry lay in his conviction that when all else fails,
God never fails (16:19 to 17:27).

## When Prayer Fails: No Intercession Permitted (14:1 to 15:9)

Do situations arise and events occur before which prayer is
powerless? One of the more difficult aspects of Jeremiah's pessimistic passages is the prohibition of prayer which is identified so clearly here in 14:1 to 15:9 and in 7:16; 11:14. Perhaps
an analysis of Jeremiah's prohibition of prayer will clarify four

factors: (1) prayer's place in human need (14:1-6), (2) the role of prophetic confession and supplication in effective prayer (vv. 7-10), (3) an assessment of times and circumstances when prayer is prohibited (14:11 to 15:4), and (4) a rationale for the failure of prayer and renewal (15:5-9).

## The Place of Prayer in Human Need (14:1-6)

Often, dynamic prayer flows from human need. To common attributes of prayer such as praise, adoration, thanksgiving, and confession, the elements of petition and intercession should be added as primary qualities. This is not to suggest that prayer is no more than suffering people's last resort; we must recognize that often, the desperation of human situations drives people to God as the ultimate source of deliverance.

Jeremiah's prayer (14:7-10) and its prohibition (vv. 11-12) emerged in the context of a severe drought throughout the land. Natural phenomena such as droughts often were interpreted as media of revelation which expressed divine judgment. In referring to natural phenomena, we should remember that the Old Testament language had no word for "nature." The Hebrews could not have said "nature" had they wanted to do so; they only could say "God." Their view of causality presupposed that he was responsible directly for all events.

The devastation and the extent of the drought were apparent everywhere (vv. 1-6). The drought was so severe that people lamented and cried (v. 2). Cisterns were empty, and servants returned to their nobles confounded because no water was available (v. 3). The land was personified and described as "dismayed"; farmers covered their heads, probably in lamentation (v. 4). Even cattle forsook the newborn calves (v. 5), and wild asses so accustomed to sparse provisions panted for air like jackals; their eyes failed because no herbage was to be found (v. 6). This was the context in which the prophet's prayer emerged (vv. 7-10). Such desperate circumstances as those Jeremiah described underscore the fact that human need becomes the matrix for authentic prayer.

## Prophetic Confession and Supplication (14:7-10)

The structure and content of Jeremiah's prayer are models which well might shape contemporary prayer. Confession (v. 7) always ought to precede supplication (vv. 8-10), while supplication should be grounded in who God is (vv. 8-9). If God is to act in the context of human need, persons' ultimate hope is that he will act despite their sin and because of his name's sake (v. 7).

1. *Confession* was the logical point of beginning in the prophet's prayer (v. 7). He acknowledged that people's lives were bent or twisted from the norm ("iniquities," *'awon,* v. 7) and that they had missed the mark set by the Lord in the covenant ("sinned," **hata',** v. 7). Also, their "backslidings" or turning back (**meshuboteynu,** v. 7) were many. Such a threefold confessional opened the possibility of prayer to the Lord of the covenant. Given sin's reality and people's unworthiness, the ground of hope in prayer was that the Lord would " 'act . . . for . . . [his] name's sake' " (v. 7).

2. *Supplication* followed confession in Jeremiah's prayer. It was grounded in who God is and the impact of his character on the human situation (vv. 8-9a). Jeremiah used two positive characterizations of the Lord followed by four negative implications of any possible refusal by the Lord to respond. Such supplication found its basis in the honor and sanctity of the Lord. He was the " 'hope of Israel, its savior in time of trouble' " (v. 8a). For the Lord to fail to act would be to suggest that he was like a " 'stranger in the land, like a wayfarer who . . . [turned] aside to tarry for a night' " (v. 8). Yet the relationship between the people and the Lord was based on a more permanent basis than was implied by the terms " 'stranger' " and " 'wayfarer.' "

Also, for the Lord to fail to act was to imply that he was unable to resolve the situation: " 'Why shouldst thou be like a man confused? like a mighty man who cannot save?' " (v. 9). So God's honor was at stake during such intercessory prayer. Should the Lord fail to deliver his people, other people might question the honor of Judah's deity. God acted through prayer not only because of human need but because of who he was. Also, he acted because of what responding or failing to respond suggested about his relationship to the people of the covenant. Although such obligations were self-assumed, the covenant not only imposed stipulations for persons; it also implied responsibilities for the Lord. This factor clarifies Jeremiah's final appeal. The Lord should act because of who Judah was: " 'We are called by thy name; leave us not' " (v. 9). The people called by his name had a legitimate claim on the Lord's sustaining power.

## Prohibition of Prayer (14:11 to 15:4)

Few phrases are stranger to those who believe in prayer's legitimacy and power than, "The Lord said to me: 'Do not pray for the welfare of this people' " (v. 11). Three themes shape the structure of Jeremiah's larger discussion of the prohibition of prayer: No prayer was permitted (vv. 11-12); no excuses were accepted (vv. 13-16); and the time had passed to pray (14:17 to 15:4).

*No prayer for the people's welfare was permitted (vv. 11-12).*—In discussing previous passages which prohibited prayer for Judah, explanations were attempted for such strange prohibitions. (See Jer. 7:16; 11:14.) Three factors emerge in verses 11-12 which may assist each reader in understanding the removal of prayer from the prophet's speech. All prayer was not prohibited, only prayer for the people's welfare. The command did not ban all forms of prayer. It was the refusal to set aside the Lord's decree of judgment. The drought was an expression of divine judgment which would not be suspended. Judgment had to be borne and could not be removed from human experience no matter how much others interceded.

Furthermore, Jeremiah had discussed the people's shallow worship and the false bases on which they sought to establish their relationship with the Lord. We should not be surprised, therefore, that God said: " 'Though they fast, I will not hear their cry, and though they offer burnt offering and cereal offering, I will not accept them' " (v. 12). One person cannot pray another into a right relationship with God. The other person must enter that relationship out of the volition of his or her will; without such personal renewal and turning to the Lord, a person's cry will not be accepted. Still further, the consequences of sin and rebellion work havoc in a person's life; once they are set in motion, they cannot be recalled. Sin's results are inevitable, even though sin may be forgiven.

*No excuses for the people were accepted (vv. 13-16).*—Knowing that the people had been misled by the false prophets, Jeremiah appealed to that fact as a basis for excusing Judah's conduct: "Ah', Lord God, behold, the prophets say to them' " (v. 13). The Lord acknowledged this fact freely (v. 14). But those prophets who spoke of peace and the assurance that sword and famine would not come on the land would die by those same realities (v. 15). Yet the prophets' failure did not exempt the people: " 'And the people . . . shall be cast out of the streets of Jerusalem' " (v. 16).

*The Lord's word presupposes that the time had passed to pray (14:17 to 15:4).*—The devastation of warfare was to be seen everywhere (vv. 17-18). Jeremiah wept as he beheld the disaster which he, in large measure, ascribed to false prophets and priests (v. 17). For those religious leaders, ministry had become only a trade: " 'For both . . . ply their trade through the land' " (v. 18). More serious than that, they functioned as religious leaders although they had no experiential knowledge of the Lord (v. 18). When religious leaders had degenerated and the destruction of the nation was a reality, prayer was too late.

In a passage much like the intent of verses 7-10, Jeremiah again turned to intercession and petition. The two prayers underscore the primacy of prayer for Jeremiah. Also, they show the gravity of God's rejecting Jeremiah's prayer.

Jeremiah's prayer consists of questions, affirmations, and exhortation. The interrogative mood is clear: "Hast thou utterly rejected Judah? Does thy soul loathe Zion? Why hast thou smitten us so that there is no healing for us?" (v. 19a). Jeremiah also affirmed the disappointment of people who looked for peace but for whom no good came, of those who sought healing but discovered terror (v. 19). Such affirmation turned to a form of confession as he acknowledged corporate sin: "We acknowledge our wickedness, . . . the iniquity of our fathers, for we have sinned against thee" (v. 20). On the basis of both question and affirmation, the prophet exhorted God to act: "Do not spurn us . . . ; remember and do not break thy covenant" (v. 21). In addition to his appeal to covenant fidelity and God's honor (v. 19), Jeremiah affirmed people's absolute dependence on the Lord: "Are there any among the false gods of the nations that can bring rain? Or can the heavens give showers?" (v. 22). To this, Jeremiah added his closing appeal. Only the Lord could help Judah in her time of need: "We set our hope on thee" (v. 22).

Stirring in its content and vibrant in the faith it manifests, Jeremiah's prayer remains a model for intercession. Yet the Word of the Lord remained the same. The time had passed for prayer. Referring to two of the renowned intercessors in Israel's history—Moses and Samuel—the Lord affirmed that even if they stood before him, his heart would not turn toward his people (15:1). The fault lay with neither Jeremiah nor the quality of his prayers; it lay with the people. Sin's results always run their course: " 'Send them out of my sight, and let them go!' " (v. 1). Should a person ask where the people were to go, the answer would be terse and graphic: to pestilence, sword, and famine—three dreaded factors of warfare. Judah had sinned away her day of grace.

## Why Prayer Fails (15:5-9)

The negative answer to Jeremiah's intercessory prayer should be interpreted in the context of his request that the people be delivered so that they might know "good." The Lord's answer to Jeremiah sprang from the fact that prayer cannot void judgment. Only repentance and commitment in the context of the covenant could void judgment and restore a broken relationship. Jeremiah's rhetorical question isolated the pathetic condition of a nation for whom prayer was too late: " 'Who will have pity on you . . . or who will bemoan you? Who will turn aside to ask about your welfare?' " (v. 5). Normally, a person would assume that the Lord would manifest such interest and concern; but Jeremiah offered four reasons why God was unable to respond to Judah's moment of crisis. (1) Judah had rejected the Lord (v. 6a). (2) The Lord said, "You keep going backward" (v. 6b). (3) The Lord was "weary of relenting" (v. 6c). The Lord was tired of the constant cycle of sin, forgiveness, restoration, and sin. (4) Despite the fact that the Lord continually "winnowed" them in the events of history (v. 7), they did not respond. Not even the disaster of warfare brought Judah to her senses (vv. 8-9).

# When the Prophet Fails (15:10-21)

Chapters 11—20 contain intimate glimpses of Jeremiah's inner life which have been called his confessions. However a person might title those passages, they vividly portray Jeremiah's moments of deep discouragement, culminating in the account of his effort to abandon the prophetic office (20:7-18). Numerous factors contributed to Jeremiah's struggle, not the least of which was the fact that he was drafted as a prophet somewhat against his will (1:4-7). Also, the prophet was disappointed at Josiah's premature death and the fate of Josiah's reform movement upon Jehoiakim's succession. Jeremiah was betrayed by friends and relatives (11:18-20), and his message was one of "strife and contention" (15:10). When he foretold the fall of Jerusalem, it seemed destined never to arrive. But when the city did fall, it required two historical events which were separated by ten years. The wicked always seemed to prosper, no matter what the emphasis on reformation might have implied (Jer. 12). The Lord even rebuffed Jeremiah's prayers (14:11 to 15:4). Those who listened to Jeremiah questioned whether the Lord would do anything, good or evil (5:12; 17:15). Against this background, should anyone be surprised that Jeremiah believed he had failed? To understand Jeremiah's experience and to learn from it, an individual might consider the prophet's failure (vv. 10-14), the prophet's protest (vv. 15-18), and the unfailing Lord (vv. 19-21).

### The Prophet's Failure (15:10-14)

In language that is reminiscent of Job (compare Job 3), Jeremiah lamented the day of his birth: "Woe is me, my mother, that you bore me" (v. 10). Jeremiah's personality probably was different from the nature of his message, for he took no delight in being "a man of strife and contention" (v. 10). Yet this was his reputation because of the message that the Lord had placed on his lips. (See Jer. 1:9.) Reflecting on the ill reputation gained by both lenders and borrowers, Jeremiah said: "I have not lent, nor have I borrowed, yet all of them curse me" (v. 10). The prophet called on the Lord to attest that he had "entreated . . . [the Lord] for their good . . . pleaded with . . . [him] on behalf of the enemy" (v. 11). Yet one could no more break the power of history over Judah than one could break iron and bronze (v. 12). The fault was not Jeremiah's, for he interceded for the people.

Few human responses are as discouraging as the failure to read one's motives correctly. Jeremiah was accused of being a man of strife and contention, but actually he had prayed for Judah's welfare. If fault was to be assessed, it was not Jeremiah's but the Lord's. The Lord had declared: " 'Your wealth and your treasures I will give as spoil, without price, for all your sins. . . . I will make you serve your enemies in a land which you do not know' " (vv. 13-14). Yet Jeremiah was the one who bore the brunt of Judah's accusation, not the Lord! Misunderstood and rejected by those whom he loved and for whom he prayed, Jeremiah experienced the depths of pessimism marked by apparent failure. He was the portrait of a devout prophet who served God faithfully, devoted to his calling, only to experience disillusionment and despair.

## The Prophet's Protest (15:15-18)

In protesting his treatment, Jeremiah stated the basis for his complaint (vv. 15-17) and questioned his future with the Lord (v. 18). Jeremiah believed that he had adequate grounds for his protest. He assumed that people's ways were known to the Lord (v. 15) and that, since the Lord knew, he would act responsibly in dealing with the prophet's appeal. "Remember me and visit me," he pled; "take vengeance for me. . . . take me not away; . . . know that for thy sake I bear reproach" (v. 15). Not only had Jeremiah acted for the Lord's sake (v. 15), he had responded positively to the Lord's word. He had been obedient to that word; it had become the joy and delight of his life (v. 16). Because of the nature of his message and his symbolic actions, he neither sat in the company of merrymakers nor rejoiced; he sat alone (v. 17). The prophet's fidelity was beyond question.

Given the nature of his response to the Lord's word, indeed his total life as described in verses 15-17, Jeremiah's question was all the more pertinent. "Why is my pain unceasing. . . . Wilt thou be to me like a deceitful brook?" (v. 18). That Jeremiah's pain had been "unceasing" and his "wound incurable" was expressed throughout the record of his words. Jeremiah felt betrayed. In response to his faithfulness to the Lord's word, he had suffered massive rejection by people. Thus, he believed that the Lord had abandoned him "like a deceitful brook."

## The Unfailing Lord (15:19-21)

Many discouraged people may believe that the Lord has abandoned them to others' misunderstanding; however, Jeremiah discovered that the Lord is unfailing. Yet, his reacceptance and strength were conditioned by his return to the Lord coupled with the ability to distinguish between what was precious and what was worthless (v. 19). If Jeremiah returned (*shub,* a common word for *penitential return*), God assured him: " 'I will restore you, and you shall stand before me' " (v. 19*a*). Jeremiah and his prophetic successors who uttered what was precious would be as God's mouth (v. 19). People endowed with the Lord's presence (v. 20) have his assurance of ultimate triumph: " 'They shall turn to you' " (v. 19). Of those who opposed the prophet, God said: " 'They shall not prevail over you' " (v. 20). Not only would the Lord deliver Jeremiah from the hand of the wicked, he would redeem him from the ruthless

(v. 21). The Lord's response to Jeremiah's pessimism reaffirmed the prophet's call experience.

Jeremiah's remaining hope rose from a faith that was strong enough to leave the validation of his ministry to the unfolding future. Today, as in every age, to live with no guarantee of success but with the conviction of the rightness of one's commitments rests at the heart of authentic commitment. Time vindicated Jeremiah. Such vindication by later history was reflected amply in the answer to Jesus' question: " 'Who do men say that the Son of man is?' And they said ... 'and others Jeremiah' " (Matt. 16:13-14).

## When the People Fail (16:1-18)

The theme of Judah's failure emerges once again in verses 1-18. Through symbolic action, the prophet communicated the threat of impending disaster (vv. 1-9); through words, he communicated the themes of rejection and restoration (vv. 10-18).

### Prophetic Symbolism of Doom (16:1-9)

Prophets communicated their messages through words and symbolic acts. Through a life-style commanded by the Lord, Jeremiah embodied the joyless despair which would befall the nation.

1. Jeremiah was prohibited to marry in order to underscore the calamitous state of the destroyed land (vv. 1-4). Through his rejecting marriage, Jeremiah pictured the solitary, lonely life; but more than that, he sought to depict the awesome nature of the future. Children and wives would die of triple threats in the siege: disease, sword, and famine (v. 4). Jeremiah's rejecting marriage was neither a commentary for others to follow nor a model for people to implement today, any more than it was for him a form of monastic celibacy. It was a symbolic act which portrayed the desperate conditions which Judah faced in the nation's collapse.

2. Jeremiah rejected all forms of lamentation and celebration as he tried to communicate Judah's comfortless condition (vv. 5-8). Verses 5-6 refer to the common rites of lamentation.

### Punishment Precedes Restoration (16:10-18)

Jeremiah restated the rationale for judgment through exile. The question-and-answer method was a form of communication common to Deuteronomic influence. (Compare Deut. 6:20). Questions deliberately were posed in order to permit a theologically oriented answer. The people did not know why calamity had come upon them. This seemed to question Jeremiah's preaching and its validity, for he often returned to that theme. Jeremiah raised the questions in verse 10 in order to give the proper answer in verses 11-13. Judgment had overtaken Judah because the people had forsaken the Lord, gone after and worshiped other gods, refused to keep the law, and refused to listen to the Lord.

Restoration was possible beyond judgment (vv. 14-15). Jeremiah compared the Lord's action to a new Exodus. He indicated that people would marvel at the Exiles' return as once they had marveled at the Exodus from Egypt.

To avoid any misunderstanding which might have been caused by the word of grace in verses 14-15, a second statement focused on punishment as the condition for Judah's being accepted again (vv. 16-18). The threat that the Exiles would receive double " 'recompense [for] their iniquity and their sin' " (v. 18) is echoed later in the introduction to the deliverance of Exiles: "She has received from the Lord's hand double for all her sins" (Isa. 40:2).

## When All Else Fails: Then, God Is There (16:19 to 17:27)

What remains when prayer (14:1 to 15:9), the prophet (15:10-21), and the people (16:1-18) have failed? When all else fails, the Lord who never fails still remains. The poetic form of Jeremiah 16:19-21 introduces a new thrust in the prophet's message and focuses on the ultimate triumph of people whose confidence rests in God (16:19-21). Following this is an extended statement on the Lord as the hope of Israel (17:1-27).

### Confidence and Ultimate Triumph (16:19-21)
Confidence adequate to transform Jeremiah's moment of despair came because of his reliance on the Lord and his conviction that beyond the shadows of the approaching Exile, individuals would respond to the Lord. Despite the traumatic nature of the times, the prophet lost confidence neither in God nor in the final commitment of people. Confidence in the Lord was genuine because Jeremiah believed that the Lord was his

strength, his stronghold, and his refuge in the days of trouble (v. 19). His confidence in the people came out of their actions and their proclamations. Jeremiah believed that someday, the people would come to the Lord "from the ends of the earth" (v. 19). As they came, they would affirm the integrity of God who, as Lord, is the only God.

### The Lord, the Hope of Israel (17:1-27)

Hope rests in the fact that God is and that he is for us. Jeremiah believed in God's existence and in God's presence with persons. In his affirming people's dependence on the Lord, Jeremiah isolated their hopelessness (17:1-11) counterbalanced by the Lord as their hope (vv. 12-18).

*The hopelessness of persons (vv. 1-11).*—Earlier, Jeremiah indicated that a person can be so bound by sin that doing good is impossible. (Compare 13:23.) In passages that reflected a similar theology (vv. 1-11), the prophet described persons' hopelessness from four perspectives.

1. Persons' hopelessness rested in the depth of their sin (vv. 1-4). Sin cannot be ignored as a fundamental source of hopelessness. This is reflected in sin's ingrained depth and in its location within the heart (v. 1). Jeremiah said: " 'The sin of Judah is written with a pen of iron; with a point of diamond it is engraved' " (v. 1). Indelibly inscribed, sin dominates the heart. For the Hebrew, the heart was not the seat of emotion but of intellect and will. It was the center of life where volitional decisions occurred. Exile and its destructive effects described in verses 2-4 were the direct consequence of sin: " 'All your treasures I will give for spoil as the price of your sin' " (v. 3). Jeremiah used the common word for **sin** meaning to *miss the mark*; elsewhere, Old Testament writers described it as a rebellion, a bending or twisting from a norm or standard.

2. Persons' hopelessness rested in misplaced confidence (vv. 5-8). In a passage reminiscent of Psalm 1, Jeremiah contrasted the person who was cursed (vv. 5-6) and the person who was blessed (vv. 7-8). In both instances, the polarities between the two were described in terms of people who trust in people (v. 5) and people who trust in God (v. 7). A person who trusts in people is " 'like a shrub in the desert, and shall not see any good come. He shall dwell in the parched places of the wilderness' " (v. 6). Contrasted with this person is the one who trusts in the Lord (v. 7), who is " 'like a tree planted by water' " (v. 8).

3. Persons' hopelessness rested in the deceitfulness of the human heart (vv. 9-10). For Old Testament persons, the heart was the point of decision-making. With such a function, if the heart is not dependable, we should not be surprised that people face hopelessness and despair. Jeremiah affirmed three things about the heart. It is "deceitful," "corrupt," and beyond understanding (v. 9). "Deceitful" is from the verb (**ya'qob**) related to the personal name Jacob. Like Jacob's deceitfulness with Esau, the heart will deceive you.

4. Persons' hopelessness rested in the instability of their lives without God (v. 11). Fewer passages more graphically illustrate the instability of life than Jeremiah's analogy of the partridge: "Like the partridge that gathers a brood which she did not hatch, so is he who gets riches but not by right; in the midst of his days they will leave him, and at his end he will be a fool" (v. 11). Its location in the book of Jeremiah gives to it a larger purpose which transcends riches alone. Placed in the context of people's relationship to the Lord, the analogy suggests the instability of the life which rests in riches rather than in the Lord.

*The Lord: Hope of Israel (vv. 12-18; see also vv. 7-11).*—In the context of despair, Jeremiah described the Lord as "the hope of Israel" (v. 13). To affirm the Lord as the focus of hope was not new with Jeremiah. Yet, he contributed significantly to a deeper understanding of that hope as he described its character.

1. The Lord is persons' hope because he alone deals effectively with ingrained sin (vv. 1-4). "Your wealth and all your treasures I will give for spoil as the price of your sin" (v. 3). Although not stated, the assumption is that a nation's defeat at the hand of her enemies is penalty for sin. Such anguish was a horrendous means to victory; however, this was not the last time that suffering would become the avenue to atonement.

2. The Lord is persons' hope because he alone is worthy of ultimate confidence (vv. 7-8). In contrast to people who placed their confidence in human beings (v. 5) and the barren life which this generated (v. 6), those who trusted in the Lord would find a benediction in life: " 'Blessed is the man who trusts in the Lord' " (v. 7). Such a person is like a tree planted by water.

3. The Lord is persons' hope because he alone properly evaluates the heart (vv. 9-10). Although people may judge by

externals, " 'the Lord looks on the heart' " (1 Sam. 16:7). Although no one can understand the heart (v. 9), God said: " 'I the Lord search the mind and try the heart' " (v. 10). Not only so, but the Lord judges persons correctly (v. 10). Only the Lord can reveal to people their true needs and ultimate values. Only he can inspire and motivate their wills so that they commit their lives to him.

4. The Lord is persons' hope because he alone assures stability (vv. 12-13). People whose riches disappoint them like the departing brood of a partridge experience instability. By contrast, the stability of people bound in relationship with the Lord rests in "a glorious throne set on high from the beginning" (v. 12). For them, the Lord is "the hope of Israel" despite all who may forsake him as the "fountain of living water" (v. 13).

5. The Lord is persons' hope because he alone is the source of healing and help (vv. 14-18). Jeremiah affirmed the Lord as his "praise" in life (v. 14). He called to the Lord for deliverance and help: "Heal me, O Lord, and I shall be healed; save me, and I shall be saved" (v. 14). Pressed by accusing countrymen, Jeremiah saw in the Lord One who was his "refuge in the day of evil" (v. 17). Some individuals apparently accused Jeremiah of having sought their evil, for he asked the Lord to witness that he had not pressed God to send evil; he had not desired the day of disaster (v. 16). Yet the prophet's message was a strange mixture of intercession and condemnation. For in the same larger context in which he affirmed that he had not pressed the Lord to send evil, he concluded by asking God: "Bring upon them the day of evil; destroy them with double destruction" (v. 18). Jeremiah may have distinguished between what he actually wanted for the people and what circumstances dictated for them. The passages' total thrust remains clear; Jeremiah discovered in the Lord the hope of Judah because of the nature of the Lord's covenant relationship with people.

## The Lord, Hope of Israel, Demands Sabbath Observance (17:19-27)

Initially a person may think that such a moving, poetic statement on people's hope, followed by a prosaic statement on sabbath observance, is strange. That the material is different in style can be observed by consulting the poetic and prose distinctions in the Revised Standard Version.

Given Jeremiah's attitude toward worship practices, that the present material has been placed in the text as a means of counteracting the flagrant abuses associated with worship is understandable. These likely included superficial attitudes toward the sabbath. The material also suggests that people's response to God makes use of structured patterns to implement their devotion to God. Central to the covenant was the assumption that time belonged to God, a reality symbolized by returning the seventh day to him. By restoring that day to its primal condition—no work done by worshipers—people testified that the day and, in turn, all time uniquely belonged to God.

More specifically, within the present text, the sabbath passage illustrates the way in which Judah rejected the Law and abused the sabbath (vv. 19-23). It also embodies positive results of sincere observance of the sabbath (vv. 24-27).

In bold relief, Jeremiah fixed his hope in the Lord. The heart deceives, confidence in self fails, and persons confess their total inability to rise unaided from sin's power. With Jeremiah, people today discover in the Lord their only hope. With him, people cry:

> Heal me, O Lord, and I shall be healed;
> save me, and I shall be saved.—Jeremiah 17:14

## Lessons for Life from Jeremiah 14—17

*Above all else, Jeremiah teaches contemporary persons that no matter what else may fail in life, God never fails.*—As was true with the prophet, so every generation experiences times when prayer seems to fail. Religious leaders or even God's people corporately fail. In such times of disintegration, when stabilizing powers which have been supportive for so long fail, people ask again: What remains now? The response doubtless will appear simplistic to some and extremely naive to others. Yet people are neither simplistic nor naive to affirm that when all support systems have failed and when even the most personal of devotional responses seem ineffective, God remains to strengthen and sustain them. Indeed, in the loss of all support other than God, people may be driven to a purity of faith otherwise inaccessible apart from the loss of external supports.

*The centrality of prayer for the life of faith continues to be crucial for believers.*—On occasions, Jeremiah prayed for the people; on other occasions, he prayed for himself. But in all instances, his prayers consisted of conversations with God.

More than merely conversing with God, however, he often argued with him. He challenged the equity of God's dealings or protested God's failure to restore Judah. Whatever the focus of Jeremiah's prayers, their genuine nature as conversations with God shines through all their varied forms.

*Crises beyond immediate human resolution form the central core of intercessory prayer.*—For contemporary believers as for Jeremiah, the extremity of human need underscores the priority of prayer in facing crises. No easy answers may be offered to explain intercessory prayer's effectiveness. Rational explanations fall in the face of ultimate mystery, and in a modern era a person may be baffled at such intercession. Yet despite one's inability to explain prayers of intercession, persons repeatedly intercede on behalf of others facing ultimate crises. Jeremiah remains to challenge today's believers to a life of intercession.

# Personal Learning Activities

1. Dr. Honeycutt gave six attributes of prayer. List three of those attributes.

2. From Jeremiah's experience, we learn that the moment never comes when intercession is too late. True _____ False _____

3. According to Dr. Honeycutt, Jeremiah's prayer remains a model for _____ . (Choose the correct answer from the list.)
   (1) Thanksgiving          (3) Praise
   (2) Supplication          (4) Intercession

4. Through the symbolism of _____ , Jeremiah showed the joyless despair that would befall Judah. (Select the proper response from the list.)
   (1) A parable             (3) His life-style
   (2) Sackcloth and ashes   (4) Weeping

5. Jeremiah compared Judah's restoration beyond judgment to (choose the correct response from the list):
   _____(1) A military          _____(3) David's reign
            victory
   _____(2) A new Exodus        _____(4) A new Temple

66

# 5

# Beginning Again

## Jeremiah 18—20

He reworked it into another vessel, as it
seemed good to the potter to do.—Jeremiah 18:4

Second only to the gift of life is the gift of a second chance which brings with it the opportunity for correcting previous errors. Not all persons want another opportunity. For those who might receive such a gift, no guarantee is given that they will act more wisely the second time. Yet, most persons have moments when they wish that they could repeat parts of their lives. Such a gift was offered to Judah. Jeremiah saw a potter working in the south end of Jerusalem one day. God impressed him to observe the potter rework the clay which had been mis-shaped in his hands and to conclude that the Lord could re-shape Judah.

The story of the potter takes on added significance because of its place in the book of Jeremiah. It follows the so-called pessimistic passages of Jeremiah 11—17 in which Jeremiah concluded that prayer, the prophet, and the people had failed. Therefore, the people had rejected the covenant and the efforts toward renewal (Jer. 11—13). By its location, chapter 18 af-firmed that God would begin again. He would rework the mis-shaped clay into another vessel as would seem good to the Potter, if only Judah would respond as clay in the potter's hands.

Chapters 18—20 should be treated as a single unit. They are bound together by common concerns with the opportunity of a new beginning. Such an opportunity was extended to Judah in chapter 18, but chapter 19 contains an emphasis on the limits to such opportunities. According to chapter 20 the prophet experienced a renewal of his call experience, for he had reached the depths of despair and contemplated rejecting the prophetic office (20:9). A person may consider those themes from these perspectives: beginning again, the moment of opportunity (18:1-23); beginning again, too late (19:1-15); beginning again, life's second chance (20:1-18).

## Beginning Again: The Moment of Opportunity (18:1-23)

While the story of the potter may not be a parable by formal definition, it has the marks of a parable. The life-centered basis for the truth communicated and the way in which parables lead to self-indictment are primary. The truth that Jeremiah communicated was obvious for anyone to understand: God would give Judah a second opportunity. Such an emphasis was predicated on the assumption that God related to people with freedom that altered his action in the context of their response. The moment of opportunity had come a second time for the people of God.

### Revealing a Transcendent Purpose Through God's Providence (18:1-12)

When Jeremiah observed the potter working at his wheel, he perceived two truths. First, as people and nations become clay in God's hands, he will make their lives vessels suitable for his purposes. Second, when the purposes for persons' or nations' lives are marred, God can rework those lives according to another purpose.

*Meeting God in the common places (vv. 1-4).*—The way in which God meets a person in the common places of life is remarkable. Moses, tending sheep in a Midianite wilderness, met God at a desert bush (Ex. 3). Gideon was beating out wheat in the winepress (Judg. 6:11); Saul was coming from the field behind his oxen (1 Sam. 11:5). Each man had a unique experience related to God's claim on his life. So in Jeremiah's case, the word of the Lord came to him through a common place—a potter's house—where he observed the relationship of potter and clay. Yet God has the strangest way of transforming a person's common places into holy places as he fills those places with his presence.

*Meaning through divine providence (vv. 5-6).*—Often, the emphasis in the story of the potter has been placed on the fact that persons and nations are clay in God's hand (vv. 5-6). To stop with this truth is to miss the larger purposes suggested in the account of the potter's work (vv. 3-4) and in the interpretation of those events (vv. 7-11). The climax of the potter's action came as the "clay was spoiled in the potter's hand, and he reworked it into another vessel, as it seemed good to the potter to do" (v. 4). The Revised Standard Version translates the Hebrew text as "he reworked it into another vessel," but the Hebrew uses two verbs as opposed to the one used in the Revised Standard Version. The phrase might be translated: And he turned [from **shub,** the word used by Jeremiah to describe *a change of direction*], and then he proceeded to make [of] it another vessel just as was right [proper] in the eyes of the potter.

The point is, God changes his intention in the light of people's failure. Stated otherwise, God's purposes for persons are pliable. He expects people to be as pliable as clay in his hands. God's providence functions in human life in such ways that life can be shaped by purposes which transcend people's agenda.

*Mystery of a double freedom (vv. 7-10).*—In the Hebrew text of Jeremiah, verses 5-12 have been identified as a series of couplets: 5-6, 7-8, 9-10, 11-12. The two sets of verses in verses 7-10 (7-8, 9-10) focus on twin themes.

First, if the Lord declares judgment on a nation (v. 7) and that nation "turns from its evil" (v. 8), the Lord will "repent of the evil that . . . [he] intended to do to it" (v. 8). The word **evil (ra')** can mean *calamity;* such meaning applied here eliminates the moral problem associated with God's turning from evil. Calamities are evil only when moral judgments are extended to them. Also when the Lord used the word **repent**, it suggested *a change of purpose* and had none of the connotations of moral reformation often associated with the English word *repent*. In fact, the same Hebrew word **(naham)** is used for "comfort" in Psalm 23:4. It is a word for emotion and will. It suggests internal alteration of intent as opposed to external moral redirection.

Second, if at any time God declares good for a nation or a kingdom, and the persons do evil in his sight, then he said, " 'I will repent of the good which I had intended to do' " (vv. 9-10). That **"repent"** implies *alteration of purpose* and not moral redirection is suggested further in the phrase which proposes that God will "repent" of good.

People have freedom to respond to God's purposes, and God has freedom to change his purposes in the context of their responses. The parable of the potter illustrates a double freedom.

*Message of renewal and hope (vv. 11-12)*.—In such double freedom as described in verses 7-10 rests the hope of disconsolate persons who wanted to do better with their lives than they did. Somehow they made the wrong choices so that the clay had been marred in the Potter's hand. Why it was marred or what flaw emerged does not matter. Only the fact that God promised to rework the clay into another vessel, equally suitable for his purpose of service, has ultimate significance.

In verses 11-12 (which should be considered together), Jeremiah contrasted the Lord's purpose with people's pride. *First*, the Lord's purpose was clear: He was shaping evil against the nation. Yet, he was consistent with the lesson from the potter. If Judah changed her evil ways and amended her activities, the Lord would change his purposes (v. 11; compare vv. 7-10). *Second*, the people's pride was obvious in their response to the Lord's promise (v. 12). Although the word for pride does not occur, its attributes emerge in the arrogant response: " 'We will follow our own plans, and will every one act according to the stubbornness of his evil heart' " (v. 12).

Pride often has been associated with humanity's lost opportunities, as in the beginning (Gen. 3; 11:1-9). Jeremiah interpreted the attitude through verse 12 as he described the pride of lost opportunities. Brought through the providence of God to the second chance for which so many people since that day have longed, Jeremiah's people rejected their moment of opportunity.

## Responding Irrationally to One's Moment of Opportunity (18:13-17)

With Jeremiah 18:13-17, a new type of material characterized by poetic style and the customary prophetic declaration " 'Therefore thus says the Lord' " (v. 13) appears. This material affirms the essentially irrational nature of people who reject their moment of opportunity.

Three elements composed the prophet's message. *First*, through the use of a series of questions, he suggested that to reject such a moment of opportunity could not be understood and was contrary to reason (vv. 13-14). The answer to his rhetorical questions was negative. *Second*, look at the contrast of Judah's irrational action which was less reasonable than the snow or the mountain stream. The people had forgotten the Lord, worshiped other gods, stumbled in life's way, and acted so irresponsibly that they caused passersby to shake their heads in amazement (vv. 15-16). *Third*, to such senseless persons the Lord would be like the " 'east wind,' " a symbol of destruction which stood in marked contrast to the life-giving westwind that swept in from the sea (v. 17).

## Reacting Against New Challenges (18:18-23)

Responding to new challenges is not always easy. When it requires repentance and a new commitment of one's life, individuals often respond with the same fascination for the status quo as ancient Judah did.

As the people of Judah interpreted their situation, they had all that they needed: the law of the priest, the counsel of the wise, and the word of the prophet (v. 18). These factors prevented an appropriate response to the challenge of a new beginning. Yet, Jeremiah continued to threaten the people and the representatives of institutionalized religion so strongly that they plotted against him.

In his customary fashion, Jeremiah took his crisis to the Lord: "Give heed to me . . . and hearken to my plea" (v. 19). His conversation focused on himself and consisted of a question and a request. Questioning the justice of life and perhaps of God, he asked: "Is evil a recompense for good?" (v. 20). We may anticipate the answer: No, evil is not a response for good. "Yet," Jeremiah complained, "they have dug a pit for my life" (v. 20). Jeremiah's equally simple request addressed the principle of equity: "Remember how I stood before thee to speak good for them" (v. 20). Perhaps the focus of Jeremiah's request was his intercessory prayer; but whatever the context, he had sought Judah's good. Look at his reward. What justice did he receive?

Next Jeremiah's complaint assumed a form much like the imprecatory psalms, those psalms in which the psalmist cursed his enemies. Always difficult to understand, such sections of cursing and appeal for disaster to come to one's enemies testify to the depth of suffering experienced by persons of faith. The humanity of biblical figures, coupled with a commitment to justice and an appeal to equity by the oppressed, brought to the surface these strong feelings. Such curses also reflect an essential commitment to God's justice shown in historical events, however much that commitment may be diminished by the appeal for revenge on one's enemies. The larger biblical revelation exhorts people to pray for their enemies. Yet this note should be set in the larger symphony which includes other notes such as equity, justice, and the judgment within history of malignant and evil persons.

One of the hazards today's believers face when they read such sections of cursing is that of rejecting the theology of the passage because of its vindictive spirit. Should people fall prey to this temptation, they will have lost much of biblical theology's richness. They will have lost its insistence on justice, the condemnation of unrighteous action, and God's judgment within the historical process. All of this presupposes the description of that judgment in a given era's languages and patterns of expression. Jeremiah's prayer thus became a strange appeal for the starvation of children and their death by the sword, of childless and widowed wives, of men killed by pestilence and youths slain in battle (v. 21). He did not pray for their forgiveness, but he asked: "Forgive not their iniquity, nor blot out their sin" (v. 23). Praying that a marauder should come suddenly upon them (v. 22), he longed for the expression of God's anger and the overthrow of the nation (v. 23).

## Beginning Again: Too Late (19:1-15)

Judah's refusal to accept the gift of a second opportunity to become the Lord's vessel reminds me of the adage: "There are no sadder words of tongue or pen than the words, it might have been." Every potter works within a given frame of time after which nothing else can be done with a certain amount of clay. The symbolic act of the broken earthen flask was placed after the story of the potter to reaffirm the limits of opportunity. The prose narrative is straightforward and clear in meaning. It consists of two sections which focus on the dual themes of perverting God's purposes (vv. 1-9) and the finality of forsaken opportunity (vv. 10-15).

## Perverting God's Purposes (vv. 1-9)

Combining the prophetic word with the symbolic act, Jeremiah addressed some of the city elders and some of the senior priests in the Valley of Ben-hinnom, also called Topheth. (Compare 7:31; 19:6.) He reviewed the ways in which the nation had perverted God's purposes. The most repulsive aspect of their apostasy was child sacrifice. (See 7:31; 19:4-5.) The deities worshiped were strange, known neither by "their fathers nor the kings of Judah" (v. 4). Sacrifice was—and it remained—a normative aspect of worship, however much Jeremiah may have denounced its abuses. But child sacrifice always had been abhorrent. The on-site nature of the prophet's indictment doubtless intensified his assurance that the Lord would "make void the plans of Judah and Jerusalem" (v. 7). Probably Jeremiah forecast the threat of cannibalism during siege as a deliberate way of polarizing such judgment with their practice of child sacrifice: "And I will make them eat the flesh of their sons and their daughters" (v. 9).

## The Finality of Forsaken Opportunities (vv. 10-15)

After speaking to the elders and the senior priests, Jeremiah was commanded to break the earthen flask (vv. 1,10). Read verses 10-15 with bifocal vision. With part of your vision, focus on the meaning of the immediate passage apart from the larger canon of Scriptures. With the other part of your vision, focus on the significance of the sequence of chapters 18 and 19. Then ask, Why does the account of the symbolic act follow the story of the potter?

The symbolic act of breaking the earthen flask was interpreted clearly by Jeremiah: " 'So will I break this people and this city, as one breaks a potter's vessel, so that it can never be mended' " (v. 11). The reason for such destruction was neither difficult to identify nor to understand. Idolatrous worship in Topheth, the Valley of Ben-hinnom, would bring such judgment. The Lord vowed to make Jerusalem as Topheth (v. 12); that is, a place for human sacrifice as persons experienced the horror of warfare. Astral deities especially were threatening to Israel's faith, following Assyrian and Babylonian influences. Jeremiah threatened that all roofs where incense had been burned to all the host of heaven, and where drink offerings had been poured out to other gods, would be defiled. They would be defiled just as Topheth had been defiled by idolatrous worship, especially child sacrifice (v. 13). Returning to the city, Jeremiah proclaimed in the Temple the same threatening message which he had stated for the elders and the priests (vv. 14-15).

If the narrative of the broken flask had occurred elsewhere or if its meaning pertained only to a time when it circulated independently, its meaning would focus only on the breaking of the city and the nation beyond repair (v. 11). But the location of this narrative, immediately following the story of the potter, gives the account of the breaking of the potter's earthen flask added significance.

The rigidity of the earthen flask stood in marked contrast to the pliable nature of the clay so graphically described in 18:1-4. Unlike the clay in the potter's hand, the flask no longer could be changed. This was illustrated vividly once when I visited the Spode china factory in England. There, a visitor may watch the entire process of making china, including those stages at which clay marred in the production is cast into containers for reprocessing. The tourists were watching inspectors break unsatisfactory pieces just before the china was placed in firing kilns which would glaze its final form. One person in the group asked, "Can't they also be corrected?" "No," the guide answered, "there comes a time when they can only be broken." Hearing the exchange, I recalled Jeremiah's words. The tragedy of life no longer pliable beneath the touch of the master Potter is that life is broken.

"There comes a time when they can only be broken." In such rigidity, a person confronts the finality of forsaken opportunities. A rigid form of predestination which presupposes fixed segments of a person's life is not meant to be conveyed here. Yet, the time span of one's opportunity has a limit. Just as the moisture evaporates, the clay dries, and its shape is fixed, such is the finality of forsaken opportunities.

## Beginning Again: Life's Second Chance (20:1-18)

More often than not, denouncing systems of any form but especially of religion has been done at great hazard. Jeremiah quickly discovered this in the action of Pashhur the chief officer of the Temple (vv. 1-6). Despondent for a variety of reasons, Jeremiah posed the possibility of abandoning his prophetic office (vv. 7-18). Yet, when he was at the point of deepest despair and faced the actual abandonment, he discovered a second opportunity to affirm the depth of his commitment to his prophetic vocation.

## Frustrating God's Purposes (vv. 1-6)

Pashhur's treatment of Jeremiah (vv. 1-6) should be read as a continuation of the prose narrative of chapter 19, especially in view of the beginning of the poetic section in verses 7-18. Throughout, this passage shows the way in which even religious leaders may frustrate God's purposes by their commitment to the status quo and by their defense of professional interests. That the extreme action of the "chief officer in the house of the Lord" (v. 1) came after Jeremiah had taken some senior priests into the Valley of Topheth is significant. At the sites of national apostasy, the prophet had smashed the earthen potter's flask to symbolize the imminent shattering of the city. That Pashhur possessed significant power was reflected in the fact that Jeremiah was beaten and placed in the public stock (v. 2).

Jeremiah's experience serves as a warning to people who follow the prophetic style: Persons who speak and act prophetically should expect the treatment of prophets! Speaking and acting prophetically is not cultivating an immature belligerence by persons committed to their perception of God's will. Yet, that prophecy without personal sacrifice may be less than authentic remains true for every generation.

## Facing Adversity with Integrity (vv. 7-18)

How do you learn to face the disappointment, suspicion, misunderstanding, and perceived failure such as Jeremiah had while at the same time maintaining your integrity? Numerous qualities of the prophet come to mind: his stark honesty and openness with God, other persons, and himself; his unshakable conviction of divine purpose which transformed him and his situation; his commitment to the Lord, even when he did not understand God's purposes; his ability to live with contradiction and ambiguity while maintaining the positive commitments of his life. The text reveals three stages in Jeremiah's dealing with adversity: accusing God (vv. 7-8); abandoning his vocation, or hypothetically doing so (v. 9a); and accepting his dilemma creatively (vv. 9b-18).

*Accusing God: the first stage (vv. 7-8).*—Jeremiah's accusation focused on three factors: freedom, ridicule, and the content of his message.

1. Jeremiah accused God of having violated his freedom in the call experience: "O Lord, thou hast deceived me . . . ; thou art stronger than I, and thou hast prevailed" (v. 7). Jeremiah served all his days as a person drafted into the Lord's service. The call narrative validates his reluctance. (Compare 1:6.) Although he seemed to maintain freedom in that experience, in every call narrative in the Old Testament the Lord took the initiative. A person ministers with the conviction that he or she has been called.

2. Jeremiah accused God because of the ridicule he experienced in fulfilling his ministry. Such ridicule may have appeared at a variety of junctures in Jeremiah's prophesying, but one context seems especially likely: the seeming nonfulfilling of Jeremiah's prophecies. Although the ridicule was not labeled ridicule, phrases such as this would have caused him anguish: " 'Where is the word of the Lord? Let it come!' " (17:15). Most people, Jeremiah included, can survive most negative reactions from persons far better than they can accept ridicule.

3. Jeremiah accused God because of the content of his message (v. 8). As a true prophet, his message was the one God gave him (1:9; 15:16). Yet, Jeremiah had no good news to proclaim. That is, he had none that did not involve repentance, the renewal of life, and the assurance of judgment if Judah did not embody the authentic renewal of God's presence. Because of his message, the word of the Lord had become for him "a reproach and derision all day long" (v. 8).

*Abandoning one's vocation: the second stage (v. 9).*—This comment probably represents the low point of Jeremiah's ministry: "If I say, 'I will not mention him, or speak any more in his name' " (v. 9a). Apparently Jeremiah experienced such despair that he decided to abandon his prophetic role. Many people have felt like Jeremiah. Some have abandoned their calling, with an eloquent rationale but with the signals of their lives sounding retreat. This second stage of despair is crucial.

*Accepting one's dilemma: the third stage (vv. 9-18).*—People who live with disappointment and crisis in ministry but who remain by their calling have the ability to accept the dilemma of a calling. However, their rationale seldom is absolute or beyond question. They learn to live with uncertainty and ambiguity and to do so while affirming those elements of ministry about which they reasonably are certain. What they find in Jeremiah's experience forms a solid ground for maintaining their commitments: living with a transcendent purpose (v. 9), committing one's cause to God (vv. 10-12), praising God despite adversity (v. 13), learning to live with despair (vv. 14-18).

1. Living with a transcendent purpose (v. 9) enabled Jeremiah to overcome the temptation to quit, to mention God no more. The prophet said: "If I say, 'I will not mention him, or speak any more in his name,' there is in my heart as it were a burning fire shut up in my bones, and I am weary with holding it in, and I cannot" (v. 9). To stifle the purpose for which God had shaped him on the potter's wheel created a burning fire within him, one that could not be extinguished.

2. Committing his cause to God despite adversity (vv. 10-12) kept Jeremiah anchored to prophetic ministry. Jeremiah made no effort to minimize his opposition: "I hear many whispering. . . . 'Denounce him! Let us denounce him' " (v. 10). Who were these denouncers? They were his "familiar friends, watching for . . . [his] fall" (v. 10). Perhaps Jeremiah would be deceived, and his opposition could " 'overcome him, and take . . . [their] revenge on him" (v. 10). Yet Jeremiah was not deceived, and his opponents neither overcame him nor took revenge on him. Why? He had committed his cause to God (v. 12), and he had done so for three reasons. He believed that the Lord was with him (v. 11); because of this, his persecutors would not prevail. Also he believed that the Lord saw "the heart and the mind" (v. 12), both his own and those of his adversaries.

3. Praising God despite adversity (v. 13) testifies to the integrity of Jeremiah's commitments. The verse comes as a single intrusion into the larger discussion of Jeremiah's crises. Inspired by God, Jeremiah believed that praise was appropriate to his situation, for the Lord had "delivered the life of the needy from the hand of evildoers." The effect is striking: Jeremiah offered praise in the midst of opposition and question.

4. Learning to live with despair (vv. 14-18) kept Jeremiah committed to God's ministry. We approach these verses knowing that they conclude his most pessimistic passages (chaps. 11—20). With this chapter, the book leaves behind the prophet's deep discouragement and moves to other issues of covenant life. Because of this a person anticipates, here, a grand and climactic affirmation, an extended statement on God's sustaining power

or some other challenging theme. No such statements appear; only despair is present.

Jeremiah's concluding statement is a death wish so authentic that it intimidates the prophetic conception of the goodness of life. For in a passage closely akin to Job 3:3-13, in spirit and format, Jeremiah closed the chapter on his most pessimistic sayings with a disturbing fascination with death.

Neither pessimism nor fascination with death kept Jeremiah lashed to his calling. Rather, his ability to live with despair heroically bound him to that calling. He dealt directly with his feelings and voiced them, for only in expressing them could he wrestle creatively with them.

If individuals remain faithful to divine callings only when faced with no doubt, fear, despair, or pessimism, then whether or not they even should begin the journey is questionable. Persons stay by their vocations for the same reason that Jeremiah did: They learn to live with the despair which is theirs to bear. In bearing that despair, they find new sources of commitment to God who has sustained them in life's crises.

## Lessons for Life from Jeremiah 18—20

*The latent possibilities of a life touched by God's presence shape the hope of continuing generations.*—Like clay in the potter's hands, life can reflect ultimate purposes which come to reality only through God's shaping providence. Such belief in providence gives meaning to life and purpose to history. To believe that life can be more than it is can inspire some persons to live their lives with expectancy.

*God's power to reshape marred lives according to a higher purpose and to offer other avenues of service for disappointed people gives hope in the midst of failure.*—As the potter in Jeremiah's parable, God reworks the clay spoiled on life's wheel. He makes it into another vessel, equally suited for his purposes. The Potter of the universe continues to reshape and form broken lives into new patterns and mosaics.

*The gift of a second opportunity is God's promise to all people who come to him with the pliability of the potter's clay.*—Often people live as though God is unforgiving, as though he offers only one opportunity; should one fail that time, all is lost. While God's grace should not be perverted into a casual attitude toward responsibility, neither should a single opportunity's uniqueness obscure the fact that God works throughout one's lifetime.

*However patient God may be in reshaping both persons and human history, Jeremiah reminds the reader that some cannot begin again.*—In the symbolic act of breaking the flask, Jeremiah clarified the fact that occasions come when brokenness is the only alternative to a stubborn pride that rejects God's grace. Such an emphasis stands in tension with the preceding statements concerning the grace of a second opportunity. Yet, it is a contradiction born in reality. For despite the possibilities of the pliable life, times do come when the clay has hardened so that only brokenness remains as an option for God.

# Personal Learning Activities

1. Jeremiah's experience at the potter's house was intended to teach him that God is a God of (select the correct response from the list):

_____(1) Wrath                 _____(3) A second chance

_____(2) Judgment          _____(4) Easy tolerance

2. The most repulsive aspect of Judah's apostasy was (choose the proper answer from the list):

_____(1) Temple prostitution   _____(3) Family breakdown

_____(2) Neglect of sacrifice    _____(4) Child sacrifice

3. To convey the rigidity of life that results in brokenness, Jeremiah used (select the proper response from the list):

_____(1) A reed                _____(3) An iron bar

_____(2) An earthen flask   _____(4) A clay tablet

4. Match the following two lists, linking the words in the first column with the identifying phrases in the second column.

_____(1) Pashhur        (a) Beaten and placed in the stocks

_____(2) Topheth        (b) Where Jeremiah prophesied

_____(3) Jeremiah       (c) Would become like Topheth

_____(4) Jerusalem      (d) Seized Jeremiah

_____(5) Temple         (e) Valley where children were sacrificed

**Answers:** 1. (3); 2. (4); 3. (2); 4. (1)d, (2)e, (3)a, (4)c, (5)b.

# 6

# God's
# Inescapable Nearness

## Jeremiah 21—26

"Can a man hide himself in secret places so that I cannot see
him? says the Lord."—Jeremiah 23:24

God's inescapable nearness is a reality which is both reassuring and disturbing. It crashes across broken centuries and affirms God's presence in all circumstances and times. From the
beginning of the biblical revelation, inspired persons used diverse contexts and patterns of thought to affirm the centrality of
Jeremiah's finding: " 'Am I a God at hand, says the Lord, and
not a God afar off? Can a man hide himself in secret places so
that I cannot see him?' " (Jer. 23:23-24). God always is inescapable and near.

In the unavoidable meeting with God, every person hears and
experiences that inescapable nearness:

Whither shall I go from thy Spirit?
Or whither shall I flee from thy presence?
(Ps. 139:7)

With inescapable nearness, the Lord confronted the political
structure (Jer. 21:1 to 24:10), prophetic leadership (23:9-40),
and popular religion (24:1-10). God's appraisal also extended to
prophets who were faithful to his lordship (25:1-24) and whom
the people opposed because of prophetic fidelity to the Lord's
Word (26:1-24). These themes emerge into two sections in the
book of Jeremiah: the crisis of ineffective leaders (21:1 to 24:10)
and the consequences of prophetic leadership (24:1 to 26:24).

# The Crisis of Ineffective Leaders (21:1 to 24:10)

Few groups in society can rise higher than the quality of their leaders. The national leadership vacuum, especially following King Josiah's death, was evidenced by numerous Judean kings' performances. On occasion their ineffectiveness arose because of the brevity of their tenure, such as in the reigns of Jehoahaz (Shallum) and Jehoiachin (Coniah). Following Josiah's death, Jehoiakim's corruption and Zedekiah's incompetence generated Judah's crisis in leadership. Also, the false prophets were a major part of a crisis in religious leadership. Judah's prophets no longer were God's genuine spokesmen. Jeremiah scathingly denounced the false prophets' negative impact. (Compare Jer. 23:9-40.) Today, we may understand and learn from Judah's crisis of ineffective leaders by examining their political leaders, a biography of failure (21:1 to 23:8); their prophetic leaders, crisis in ministerial authenticity (23:9-40); their popular religion, the price of ineffective leaders (24:1-10).

## Political Leaders: A Biography of Failure (21:1 to 23:8)

Passages in Jeremiah other than 21:1 to 23:8 indicate his relationship with kings, especially with Jehoiakim and Zedekiah. These relationships are especially important, since in this unit sayings that related to four of the kings appear: Jehoahaz, Jehoiakim, Jehoiachin, and Zedekiah.

Before we turn to Jeremiah's discussions of ineffective political leaders, two areas should be noted. Those areas serve as background to help the reader understand Jeremiah's oracles on kingship.

*What was the normative Old Testament conception of kingship?*—Of all that might be said, these assumptions reflect the norm by which kingship should be evaluated. The king was the anointed one of God; by the act of anointing, he was set aside uniquely for God's service. This act of consecration brought the person into the realm of the holy, just as anointing consecrated places or objects related to worship. From the Hebrew verb meaning *to anoint* (**mashach**), the English noun *Messiah* is derived. The king was God's representative and should have reflected the principles of **theocracy** (*God rules*) even though the form of government had become monarchial. Also, the king was limited in power. Furthermore, the king was subject to the same moral standards that the people of his realm lived by. The kings were expected to give political and religious leadership.

Also, as reflected in the enthronement psalms (Pss. 2; 72) the king was the Lord's representative who embodied the expression of divine rule. Against these five characteristics of kingship, the quality of Judah's leadership in the political arena should be evaluated.

*More often than not, prophets stood in conflict with kingship.*—Those conflicts may be summarized in three categories. Prophets conflicted with kings over moral issues. These included violation of the Lord's commands, persecution of the prophets, oppression of the people, and—in limited instances—murderous acts.

Furthermore, prophets often stood in conflict with kings over political issues. Remember Samuel's views against kingship; Ahijah and the division of the kingdom; Isaiah's encounter with Ahaz; Jeremiah's running battle with Jehoiakim; and Jeremiah's failure to influence weak Zedekiah.

Prophets also opposed kings in the context of religious syncretism. The kings, through political expediency, incorporated foreign deities; prophets opposed the kings' action because the prophets were committed to the Lord as the true King.

Although the prophets supported the monarchy as it reflected the proper relationship to the Lord, the prophetic movement never fully abandoned Samuel's views opposing kingship. So, to discover that Jeremiah's assessment of kingship remained as a model for appraising leaders should be no surprise. Unfortunately for Judah, the crisis of ineffective leaders was so massive that it can be described as a biography of failure.

The assessment of Jeremiah's "biography of failure" focuses on twin themes: the kings' failure, despair for the present (21:1 to 22:30); and the ideal King, hope for the future (23:1-8).

The kings' failure: despair for the moment (21:1 to 22:30) summarizes the primary concerns reflected in Jeremiah's words. The Lord continued to use Jeremiah following his experience of deep pessimism (20:14-18). Jeremiah's words in 21:1 to 22:30 polarized the kings' failure with the hope for an ideal king.

Zedekiah (21:1-10) reflected a certain naive optimism as he inquired of Jeremiah when Nebuchadrezzar (an alternate form of Nebuchadnezzar) was making war against Jerusalem. " 'Perhaps the Lord will deal with us according to all his wonderful deeds, and will make him withdraw from us' " (v. 2). Zedekiah left the impression that he was an indecisive and naive weakling, unable to follow the sound word of a prophet like Jeremiah. At the other extreme, he rashly rebelled against Babylon (2 Kings 24:20). To the king (vv. 3-7) and the people (vv. 8-10), Jeremiah's counsel was one of despair. The Lord was not going to repeat his "wonderful deeds" (v. 2) of former eras; rather, God said: " ' "I myself will fight against you" ' " (v. 5). To the people, Jeremiah said: " 'He who stays in this city shall die' " (v. 9). God inspired Jeremiah to believe that true patriotism was broad enough to indict a nation for its faults and to abandon it to its appropriate judgment. However, Jeremiah's love for his country, as reflected throughout his words, never diminished.

Jeremiah isolated the normative standards of kingship as canons for judging performance (21:11 to 22:9). The first oracle (vv. 11-14) may have concerned Zedekiah and the second oracle (22:1-9) Jehoiakim. In lieu of that, the oracles are set forth as free-standing prophetic oracles on the conduct of the royal house, equally applicable to any king. The first oracle to the royal house calls for a change of policy in social justice. It links longevity and good with executing justice and delivering the oppressed from the hand of the oppressor. Furthermore, pride had to cease (vv. 13-14). The second oracle against the royal palace and the city (22:1-9) stresses the social responsibility of the king who was to " 'do justice and righteousness, and deliver from the hand of the oppressor' " (v. 3). He was to do no wrong or violence. But if he fulfilled those stipulations, he would be assured that his dynasty would continue (v. 4). If the king rejected those moral demands, he and his royal house would suffer God's wrath in history and would become a desolation (vv. 5-9).

Shallum (Jehoahaz) reigned so briefly (three months) that Jeremiah did not evaluate him as he did Jehoiakim. Rather, the prophet lamented the fate of Shallum who was taken away captive by Necho to Egypt.

In an extended lamentation, Jeremiah denounced Jehoiakim (vv. 13-23), documented his immoral activities (vv. 13-17), and characterized his fate (vv. 18-19). Of the king's building projects, which seem to have incensed Jeremiah most of all, the prophet accused him of having been guilty of unrighteousness and injustice, primarily in making his neighbor serve him for

Ruins of Jehoiakim's royal palace

nothing and in not giving him his wages (v. 13). Jeremiah further ridiculed the king's elaborate building project (v. 14) and then asked: " 'Do you think you are a king because you compete in cedar?' " (v. 15). The king had eyes and heart only for "dishonest gain, for shedding innocent blood, and for practicing oppression and violence' " (v. 17). Such a king, Jeremiah said, would die without lamentation and have the " 'burial of an ass' "—" 'dragged and cast forth beyond the gates of Jerusalem' " (v. 19).

Coniah (Jehoiachin) reigned only three months, yet Jeremiah characterized Jehoiachin (renamed Coniah by the Babylonians to show lordship over him, as the name Eliakim had been changed to Jehoiakim and Jehoahaz to Shallum) as a "despised, broken pot," a vessel no one cared for (v. 28). Even if he were " 'the signet ring on my right hand,' " said the Lord through Jeremiah, " 'yet I would tear . . . [him] off' " (v. 24). Jehoiachin was the one who came to the throne at age eighteen and in the third month of his reign surrendered to the Babylonians, bringing about the first sixth-century capture of Jerusalem.

Judah's kings were failures when measured both by normative standards of kingship and by the standards of the prophetic oracles addressed to the royal house. They comprised "a biography of failure."

The ideal King: hope for the future (23:1-8) was Jeremiah's antidote for kings' bitter failure. The term **shepherd** among Old Testament prophets was used for *political leadership*, especially in the books of Jeremiah and Ezekiel. Often, however, people tend to associate *shepherd* with a religious leader. The Old Testament thought patterns rendered impossible any significant delineation between a political and a religious leader, for even in kingships both forces were united.

Jeremiah addressed the failure of kings by describing the shepherds as irresponsible leaders who destroyed and scattered the sheep (v. 1). They had not " 'attended to them' " (v. 2); but, with an altogether different connotation, the Lord would attend to them for their evil doings (v. 2). Jeremiah said that despite this, the day was coming when the flock would be gathered again (v. 3) and shepherds set over them who would care for them; they would fear no more nor be dismayed, neither would any be missing (v. 4). In every generation, God's people hope for a good shepherd who will come to lead his people home again. Such hope was realized in the Christian faith with Jesus' work as the "good shepherd."

The ideal King would deliver the oppressed (vv. 5-8). Reference to the "righteous Branch" which the Lord would raise up affirmed the continuity of David's line. (Compare 2 Sam. 7:16.) In contrast to kings of Jeremiah's era, the ideal King would "deal wisely, and . . . execute justice and righteousness in the land" (v. 5; compare Isa. 9:7). His universal concern would include both Judah and Israel, and his name would be called "The Lord is our righteousness" (v. 6). In such a time the old Exodus, so long championed as the hallmark of God's saving grace, would be overshadowed by a new Exodus that would characterize the future deliverance of Exiles (vv. 7-8).

The crisis of political leadership (21:1 to 23:8) as "a biography of failure" would have to be rewritten. The ideal King would not fail, and someday a person could write of leaders under the theme "a biography of victory."

## Prophetic Leaders: Crisis in Genuineness (23:9-40)

The second crisis to which Jeremiah pointed was a lack of genuine spokesmen for God. False prophets emerged who had no legitimate word from the Lord and had not stood in his council; because of those failures, they had misled the people. Jeremiah's agitation with false prophets focused on their conduct (vv. 9-15). They had corrupted the land with their wickedness—both prophet and priest—in the house of the Lord (v. 11). Samaria was bad, for " 'they prophesied by Baal' " (v. 13), but Jerusalem was "horrible" (v. 14). The false prophets' personal immorality and support of immoral persons caused Jeremiah to compare them to Sodom and Gomorrah (v. 14).

Jeremiah's advice was clear: His people were not to listen to such persons (vv. 16-22). The verb **hear** in the Hebrew text (**shema'**) means both to hear and to obey. The latter connotation is applicable here: " 'Do not . . . [respond to] the words of the prophets who prophesy to you, filling you with vain hopes' " (v. 16). The unfit prophets were to be ignored for four reasons. They misled the people by filling them with false hope; they spoke their own words, not the Lord's. They condoned those who rejected the Lord's word and encouraged the person who stubbornly followed his own heart. Also, such prophets had not "stood in the council of the Lord" (vv. 18-20). The council (**sod**) of God implied the same relationship as a king and his court and apparently was well established in Old

Testament thought. Jeremiah said that if they had stood in the Lord's council, they would have spoken the Lord's word (v. 18). Because God's word had not been in or through their proclamation, God's judgment had not been isolated as a warning (vv. 19-20). Jeremiah wanted the people to remember that God had not sent those prophets (v. 21). Finally, their failure to warn the Lord's people denied them the right to be heard: " 'If they had stood in my council, then they would have proclaimed my words to my people, and they would have turned' " (v. 22). Such prophets, regardless of their era in history, have no right to a hearing with God's people.

Genuine prophets' attributes were provided as a guide for the community of faith (vv. 23-32). Genuine ministry always manifests an awareness of one's ultimate accountability to God for the impact of his/her ministry as well as its motivating power. Such a prophet is aware of God's inescapable nearness (vv. 23-24). The genuine prophet has a word from God to declare, not his own imaginations and dreams (v. 28). Old Testament prophets never felt compelled to declare the bits and pieces of their own counsel in lieu of a Word from God, not if they were authentic. They were measured by their message. Authentic prophets lived with an awareness of the nature of God's word: " 'What has straw in common with wheat? . . . Is not my word like fire, says the Lord, and like a hammer which breaks the rock in pieces?' " (vv. 28-29). The dream (straw) has nothing in common with the Word (wheat).

A person must recognize the integrity of God's Word when it is set in the context of other claims to revelation. One should remember that as the flail that separates the chaff from the wheat and as the fire that consumes the chaff, so the Lord's Word is a refining, sifting, purifying force. It is like a hammer to break the rock in pieces. It possesses power to fulfill the Lord's purposes.

Also, the genuine prophet had access to God's Word for himself and did not echo another's understanding. The true prophet had no need to borrow the words of someone else: "I am against the prophets, says the Lord, who steal my words from one another" (v. 30). Equally pertinent is the fact that true prophets did not substitute their opinions for the Lord's revelation: " 'I am against the prophets, says the Lord, who use their tongues and say, "Says the Lord" ' " (v. 31). The real prophet was marked by responsibility, not recklessness, in his relationships with the people of God (v. 32). Recklessness has no place in genuine ministry. Jeremiah associated such recklessness with "lies," and he said of that type ministry: " 'They do not profit this people at all' " (v. 32).

Jeremiah described the action to be taken against prophets who obviously lacked authenticity (vv. 33-39). With a play on the Hebrew word *massa'* which can mean either *burden* or *oracle*, Jeremiah said: "When . . . a prophet, or a priest asks you, 'What is the **burden** [*oracle*, *massa'*] of the Lord?' you shall say to them, 'You are the **burden** [*oracle*, *massa'*], and I will cast you off" ' " (v. 33). The word *burden* had been so corrupted by the false prophets that Jeremiah said: "You shall mention no more, for the burden is every man's own word, and you pervert the words of the living God' " (v. 36). Those who abused God's language by pretending to have his word or his oracle found that they were stripped of their relationship with God and were no longer to speak the oracle.

### Popular Religion: The Price of Ineffective Leaders (24:1-10)

A person can witness the costly disintegration of political and religious leaders! In Judah, the kings' failure (21:1 to 23:8) and the loss of genuine prophets (23:9-40) combined to effect the nation's collapse. Popular religion had so eroded from the norm set by covenant demands as to make continued national existence impossible. As Jeremiah had argued with the Lord when his prayers were rebuffed, the fault for the nation's decline lay primarily with the prophets who had misled the people. (Compare Jer. 14:13-18.) Yet, here as there, the faults of one person had no power to excuse another's weaknesses. People were left to bear the evil fruit of popular religion which had compromised faith and eroded commitment. Jeremiah used a common scene, baskets of figs, to characterize the fate of the people (vv. 1-3). The good figs signified the Exiles of the first deportation who would return as a part of God's purpose (vv. 4-7). The bad figs suggested the fate of the people remaining in the land and with whom Jeremiah had to deal prior to the final surrender of the nation (vv. 8-10).

The revelation of the Lord's purpose (vv. 1-3) came through the sight of two baskets of figs, one equally as good as the other was bad (vv. 1-3; vv. 4,8). Marketplaces and other common scenes often prompted the prophets' inspiration. God used common sights. At times, he used the sounds of similarity between words as in the case of the **almond tree (*shaqedh*)** and the word for **watching (*shoqedh'*)** (Jer. 1:11-12) or the **summer fruit (*qayits*)** and **the end (*qets*)** in Amos' vision (8:1-3).

The refining power of a disastrous experience (vv. 4-10) is inherent in Jeremiah's assessment of the groups that survived the surrender of Jerusalem: those who were exiled to Babylon and those who remained in the homeland. Interpreting the baskets of figs, Jeremiah indicated that the basket of good figs (vv. 4-7) were the " 'exiles from Judah' " (v. 5). A reader may have concluded that the people spared from the Exile were the favored who constituted God's hope. This was not the case. Those taken into Exile were God's hope: " 'I will set my eyes upon them for good. . . . They shall return to me with their whole heart' " (vv. 6-7). Historically, a person can trace in retrospect the creative experiences associated with the Exile: patterns of worship, forms of social relationships, and especially the theological understanding of developments during the Exile. Judaism and Christian faith would have been impoverished without the traumatic refining process of the Exile. Today, not every crisis is attended by such positive by-products. However, dynamic periods of growth in the lives of individuals and institutions often occur in moments of traumatic crisis.

The basket of bad figs (vv. 8-10), so bad that they could not be eaten, were the remnant of Jerusalem who remained in the land and those who dwelled in the land of Egypt. Those persons remained in Jerusalem during the surrender of Jehoiachin (Coniah). During the period following the surrender of Jehoiachin, Jeremiah spoke this word. He felt that those spared during the first capture of Jerusalem had no hope. His word grew out of his continued efforts to call an obstinate people to renewal— people who would not learn the lesson from history that grew out of either of the falls of Jerusalem. Those who survived the captivity as well as those who were carried into Egypt following the second surrender of Jerusalem (accompanied by Jeremiah) were destined to be " 'a horror to all the kingdoms of the earth, to be a reproach, a byword, a taunt, and a curse' " (v. 9).

The first disintegration of Jerusalem was interpreted as judgment, as was the second. Then what was the focus of the difference in Jeremiah's attitude? It seems to have been rooted in the ability of the Exiles to learn from their discipline, for they had a heart to know that God was the Lord (v. 7). The distinction between the two lay in the response to the events.

## The Consequences of Prophetic Leadership (25:1 to 26:24)

Chapters 25 and 26 are concerned with the fidelity of the prophetic office (25:1-38) and the consequences of such faithfulness manifested in the accusations brought against Jeremiah (26:1-24).

### Prophetic Faithfulness to the Lordship of Yahweh (25:1-38)

Yahweh is Lord of all life: of prophets (vv. 1-7), history (vv. 8-14), and justice (vv. 15-38). The reader is forced to use the term "Yahweh" rather than Lord which reflects a common practice in translating God's personal name as revealed to Moses. The King James Version and the Revised Standard Version use "Lord" for the God of the covenant; yet, the word Lord is used for the Lord as "sovereign." How does a person describe the Lord as Lord? Hence, the present effort to emphasize that Yahweh is Lord (sovereign).

Yahweh as Lord of the prophets (vv. 1-7) first was reflected clearly in Jeremiah's consistency or fidelity (vv. 1-3): " 'For twenty-three years . . . the word of the Lord has come to me, and I have spoken persistently to you' " (v. 3). Fewer testimonies are more eloquent to the fidelity of life than that one has received and transmitted the Lord's Word for almost a quarter of a century. The continuity of Jeremiah's message with other prophets was both a mark of validation and an added judgment on the king (v. 4). That voices other than Jeremiah's communicated the Lord's Word seems to be clear in the reference to " 'his servants the prophets' " (v. 4) While God may reveal to one person a truth never perceived by anyone else, normally one's message has internal consistency and continuity with God's other spokesmen. The content of Jeremiah's message (vv. 5-6) summarized his preaching for almost a quarter of a century. Examination of that content reveals a consistent emphasis on renewal and repentance, the contingency of the promise to the fathers, the appeal that false gods should be abandoned, and the fatal consequences of apostasy.

The consequences of Jeremiah's preaching did not deter him

from its continuation (v. 7). Stated pointedly: No one listened to him, or certainly not in sufficient numbers to alter the course of national commitments. When the rating polls place one in the upper ranks of popularity, to be faithful is not difficult. Yet, what a person does when the polls begin to fall will determine and reveal the mettle of that person's life. Jeremiah remained faithful to his calling. In twenty-three years of dedicated work, people did not believe him. But he continued to speak even as he was carried, somewhat unwillingly, by his friends into Egypt. Still, the consequences to Judah for such insensitivity to the prophetic Word were apparent: " 'that you might provoke me [God] to anger . . . to your own harm' " (v. 7).

Yahweh as Lord of history was presupposed in the description of judgment through historical processes (vv. 8-14). This passage seems to summarize the ways in which Jeremiah saw the late seventh- and early sixth-century forces of history as the arena of divine judgment. Yet, the prophets believed more than that nations and individuals merely reap what they sow, in a somewhat naturalistic manner. They were convinced that Yahweh actively participated in history. The Lord would send for "all the tribes of the north . . . and for Nebuchadrezzar the king of Babylon" (Jer. 25:9) who would come because the people had not obeyed the Lord's words (v. 8).

Yahweh as Lord of judgment emerged in the irrational conduct of Judah. The people's conduct was so senseless that it was compared with drunkenness (vv. 15-29). The judgment that Jeremiah's analogy of the "cup of the wine of wrath" described (v. 15) had a universal character, for justice is not circumscribed by nationality or personality (vv. 15-29). Hence the prophet's oracle of judgment to the nations (vv. 30-31) embraced all the "ends of the earth" and constituted an "indictment against the nations" (v. 31). That suggests an almost apocalyptic note to universal judgment. Because justice is universal, history is its medium of communication (vv. 32-38). History is not merely the measurement of time but the inner form and meaning of time (vv. 32-38). In the events of national scope, God's purposes find fulfillment, just as in the positive response of individuals.

## Prophetic Indictment and Vindication (26:1-24)

The context for Jeremiah's Temple sermon, which appears in chapter 7, was described graphically. The indictment lodged against the prophet finally was dismissed through the intervention of Jeremiah's friends. In process, the price of being a prophetic voice (vv. 1-9) and the vindication of the prophetic witness (vv. 10-24) are seen.

Questioning prophetic motivation was the essence of the people's response to Jeremiah's Temple sermon (vv. 1-9). An examination of its content (7:1 to 8:3) should show why the people reacted so violently to his declaration. Jeremiah's indictment of attitudes toward Judah's religious system as reflected in both Temple and sacrifice led everyone to question him: " 'Why have you prophesied . . . "This house shall be like Shiloh?" ' " (26:9). The question exudes enmity and hostility.

The vindication of the prophetic function was achieved by Jeremiah's friends, especially Ahikam (vv. 10-24). The priests and the prophets demanded Jeremiah's life. Accusations brought against the prophet were lodged with the "princes" of the land who apparently served as judges (v. 10). Because Jeremiah had prophesied against the city, his accusers sought the death penalty (v. 11).

The prophet's defense lay in his call: " 'The Lord sent me to prophesy' " (v. 12). The ultimate defense of any prophet rested in his conviction concerning his call and its divine origin. Also, his message was essentially the voice of the Lord God (v. 13). Finally, the prophet had reached such a point of self-surrender that his own life was of little consequence in measuring whether or not he should be faithful to God's imperative (vv. 13-14). Jeremiah suggested that the people might do as they pleased; but if they harmed him, they should be aware of two things: In harming him, they would bring innocent blood on themselves while destroying one whom the Lord sent (v. 15).

In stating his defense, Jeremiah held in balance his divine call with its attendant message and his own role. In his defense, he cast himself on the spirit of justice in those who tried him for his life. Jeremiah's deliverance came not from the priests or prophets (v. 16). Also, Jeremiah's defense rested in the fact that he had spoken in the name of the Lord (v. 16).

Referring to Micah of Moresheth who prophesied negatively against Jerusalem (v. 18), Jeremiah's defenders also appealed to prophetic tradition. Jeremiah's voice was not a single voice, isolated from the mainstream of covenant faith. He was at one with the community of faith. People may have been hostile to what Jeremiah spoke, but they knew that they had been with a prophet, as in the days of Micaiah. People knew Micaiah to be a true prophet and wanted to hear him rather than a false prophet. With evidence balanced for and against permitting a prophet to speak (vv. 20-23; 27:17-19), Jeremiah was delivered through the good influence of a single person: Ahikam.

## Lessons for Life from Jeremiah 21—26

*For many in a scientific, technological age, to believe in God's nearness is increasingly difficult.* Yet, above all else Jeremiah 21—26 affirms that no area of life lies beyond that Presence. Not easily discernible in many situations and often standing in the shadows, God permeates all creation and the full scope of human experience.

*The full range of human experience—political, religious, personal—is open to God's nearness.*—Reconciling the contradiction of God's presence and the failure of both political and religious leaders is not easy. Yet the difficulty of such reconciliation should not be allowed to obscure God's continuing presence and interaction with people as well as corporate structures. To believe in God is to bear a concurrent conviction. Life and history may run counter to God's purposes at any given moment, but an enlarging view of God sees the broader scope. A providence is at work which does not eliminate any aspect of the human situation from divine scrutiny and ultimate restoration.

*The accountability of religious leaders to God as well as the crisis in ministerial authenticity remain as crucial aspects of the faith community.*—Few biblical passages deal more pointedly and clearly with prophetic responsibility and evaluation by God than does Jeremiah's indictment of the false prophets. The loss of leaders and their attendant vacuum continue to threaten not only other corporate bodies and political systems but also the church. Into the vacuum created by the abdication of responsible leaders swirls the chaff of false leaders—or at best inept leaders—who provide no authentic Word from beyond themselves. Neither ancient Judah nor a modern-day congregation can prosper on the husks of such false prophetic leaders.

*Those who assume authentic prophetic roles in modern soci-*

ety may anticipate the fate of an ancient prophet like Jeremiah.—Jeremiah condemned the shallow emphasis on the Jerusalem Temple, and he was indicted by those who heard his Temple sermon. For people who experience criticism and opposition, deliverance seldom comes through self-defense. Rather, as in Jeremiah's case, often modern-day prophets will be delivered by friends like Ahikam who saved Jeremiah. Fidelity to God and the sustenance of friendship will continue as support systems when all else has failed.

# Personal Learning Activities

1. In Israel, the king was God's anointed representative with unlimited power. True _____ False _____
2. Match the following two lists, linking the words in the first column with the identifying phrases in the second column.
   _____(1) Zedekiah      (a) Political and religious leaders
   _____(2) Babylon       (b) Rule under God
   _____(3) Jeremiah      (c) Weak, indecisive king of Judah
   _____(4) Nebuchadrezzar(d) Often opposed kings
   _____(5) Prophets      (e) King of Babylon
   _____(6) Theocracy     (f) Advised flight from Jerusalem
   _____(7) Kings         (g) Nation threatening Judah
3. Old Testament prophets used the term shepherd for _____ _____ . (Choose the correct answer from the list.)
   (1) Political leaders    (3) Priests
   (2) Prophets             (4) Elders
4. Jeremiah used _____ to contrast the people who would be exiled and the people who would be spared from Exile.
   (1) Fruit trees          (3) Baskets of figs
   (2) Grain                (4) Clay jars

# 7

# When God Makes Plans

## Jeremiah 27—31

"For I know the plans I have for you, says the Lord."—
Jeremiah 29:11

Was Macbeth right in calling life "full of sound and fury,
signifying nothing" or "a tale told by an idiot"?[1] Contrary to
such pessimism, Jeremiah believed that God stood at the center
of history and that his plans shaped history. The late W. O.
Carver of The Southern Baptist Theological Seminary wrote of
God's "plan of the ages."[2] Jeremiah believed in God's plans
because Judah experienced God's providence in history just as
the prophet knew God's providence through his life. **Providence** literally means *to see before* (*pro* plus *videre; before* and
*see*). Because God sees before, he plans in ways consistent with
his purpose. Because of this, Jeremiah sought to lead Judah to
look beyond the fragmentation of Jerusalem's disaster to the
aftermath of Exile, and to trust God: " 'For I know the plans I
have for you, says the Lord' " (Jer. 29:11).

Conflicting counsel concerning God's plans emerged in the
debate between the false prophets of Jerusalem and Babylon
and the prophet Jeremiah (Jer. 27—29). This interchange, introduced by the phrase, "This word came to Jeremiah from the
Lord" (27:1), is followed by an exhortation to trust in God during tumultuous times (Jer. 30—31).

# Planning for the Future: Conflicting Counsel
## (27—29)

Persons do not always agree in the interpretation of God's will. That fact is clear in the conflict between Jeremiah and the prophets from Jerusalem and Babylon concerning God's plans. The prophets from Jerusalem and Babylon believed that God planned a brief exile from Jerusalem, while Jeremiah was convinced that it would last for seventy years. (Compare Jer. 28:3; 29:10.) The debate can be clarified by examining the following themes: proclaiming God's plan, Jeremiah's counsel (27:1-22); and perverting the plan of God, prophetic opposition to Jeremiah's counsel (28:1 to 29:32).

### Proclaiming God's Plan: Jeremiah's Counsel (27:1-22)

Prophetic symbolism and God's plan were intertwined in the yoke which Jeremiah wore to symbolize Judah's impending captivity (27:1-2). That action was more than an object lesson used as a teaching device. Symbolic acts, like prophetic words, were thought to set in motion the action symbolized. Jeremiah not only announced Jerusalem's fate by wearing the yoke about the streets of the city, he also was believed to have set in motion forces that eventually would bring about the captivity and the Exile.

Jeremiah's proclamation of God's plan included three groups (vv. 3-22). Jeremiah proclaimed the Lord's purposes to foreign ambassadors and, in so doing, clarified three aspects of God's plan (vv. 3-11). To the envoys of Moab, Ammon, Tyre, and Sidon who had come to consult with Zedekiah (v. 3), Jeremiah established the universality of God's creative action as the basis for God's use of Nebuchadnezzar (vv. 3-5). (Note the use of Nebuchadrezzar elsewhere.) Since it was the Lord who had made the earth, he had the right to give it to whomever he chose (v. 5). Next, Jeremiah clarified Nebuchadnezzar's sovereignty: " 'Now I have given all these lands into the hand of Nebuchadnezzar. . . . All the nations shall serve him' " (vv. 6-7).

Finally, Jeremiah emphasized that God's plan assumed surrender (vv. 8-11). Any nation which refused to submit to the Babylonian king would experience God's judgment through sword, famine, and pestilence—three classical horrors of seige (v. 8). Because of this, the people should not listen to their prophets and other religionists who were saying to them: " ' "You shall not serve the king of Babylon" ' " (v. 9). Jeremiah said that such counsel was a lie and that any nation which believed it would perish. Only by surrendering to the Babylonians could a nation be left in its own land (v. 11). That Jeremiah was declared a traitor to Judah and cast into prison (compare Jer. 32:1-5) is understandable; however, much of Judah's actions ignored the larger vision of Jeremiah's patriotism. For a depth of true patriotism exists which manifests real love of country while, under certain circumstances, it calls for national surrender. Jeremiah's hearers never understood this.

Jeremiah's proclamation was shared with Zedekiah (vv. 12-15). Jeremiah counseled him: " 'Bring your necks under the yoke of the king of Babylon, and serve him' " (v. 12). Why, Jeremiah asked, should the people die when the words of the prophets who counseled opposition to Babylon were lies (vv. 13-14)?

Jeremiah offered essentially the same counsel to the priests and to the people as he did to Zedekiah ( vv. 16-22). He stressed that Judah should surrender to Babylon; if not, the Lord would bring the forces of seige against them.

## Perverting God's Plan: Prophetic Opposition (28:1 to 29:32)

Prophetic opposition to Jeremiah's counsel (29:9,14-22) took the specific form of opposition from the prophets in Jerusalem and in Babylon.

*Difference of opinion by prophets from Jerusalem (28:1-17).*—Hananiah, a Jerusalemite prophet from Gibeon, spoke to Jeremiah in the Temple, disagreeing with his insistence that Judah should live under Babylonian domination. Within two years of Jerusalem's first surrender, Hananiah said, the vessels taken from the Temple would be returned and Jeconiah (Coniah or Jehoiachin) and all the Exiles would return. For the Lord would " 'break the yoke of the king of Babylon' " (v. 4). Jeremiah agreed with the intent of the prophecy (v. 6); yet, he warned that prophets traditionally brought messages of judgment (v. 8). Any prophecy of peace should wait for its fulfillment before people assessed its validity (v. 9).

To emphasize his point and to embody a second symbolic act, Hananiah broke the yoke which Jeremiah wore to symbolize submission to Nebuchadnezzar (28:10). By breaking that yoke, Hananiah indicated that even so the Lord would " 'break the yoke of Nebuchadnezzar' " (v. 11).

Jeremiah's patience in responding to rebuke appeared in his ability to wait before responding to criticism: "Sometime after . . . the word of the Lord came to Jeremiah" (v. 12). Not only Jeremiah's patience but the fact that he did not have automatic access to the Lord's Word was responsible for his waiting. He could not command the Word; he had to wait for its appearance. Furthermore, Jeremiah did not try to withdraw an inspired message in the face of criticism. The disagreement that Jeremiah experienced provided the context for a further declaration of the Lord's plan (vv. 13-14). Finally Jeremiah spoke to Hananiah about the danger in opposing the Lord's purposes. That hazard became real in warning (v. 16) and in Hananiah's death during the same year (v. 17).

*Difference of opinion by prophets from Babylon (29:8-9,21-32).)*—A difference of opinion by the prophets from Babylon provided the context for Jeremiah's letter to the Exiles (29:1-32). The letter was sent after Nebuchadnezzar had taken into captivity King Jehoiachin and the royal household with other leaders (vv. 1-2).

Jeremiah's letter is instructive for all persons living under adversity. He counseled the Exiles to learn to live with adversity (vv. 4-6), to settle into Babylonian life but not to be assimilated: " 'Multiply there, and do not decrease' " (v. 6). Stated for each person regardless of generation, the principle remains: Do not permit circumstances to circumscribe your life. Jeremiah told the Exiles: "Seek the welfare of the city where . . . [God has ] sent you into exile, and pray to the Lord on its behalf" (v. 7). They were to love their enemies and to pray for their welfare. They were to learn to face the truth of difficult times (vv. 8-9). Always, false prophets like Ahab and Zedekiah (v. 21) lived among the Exiles; these minimized a crisis while exploiting the situation. (Compare v. 23). Because the Exile would be longer than the leaders told the people, Jeremiah said: "Do not let your prophets and your diviners who are among you deceive you, . . . for it is a lie which they are prophesying. . . . 'When seventy years are completed for Babylon, I will visit you' " (vv. 8-10). Also, Jeremiah counseled the Exiles to experience the expulsive power of a divine commitment (vv. 12-13).

Jeremiah's letter to the Exiles clarified the reality of differences between religious leaders. Prophets in Babylon logically hoped for a brief period of Exile, quite contrary to Jeremiah's predicted seventy years. Yet their differences of opinion involved more than the length of the Exile. Jeremiah was sure of divine support for Babylon's rise to power; his prophetic opponents looked for the quick overthrow of Babylon, and they failed to include judgment in their message of hope. Jeremiah said that God's plans involved not only hope for the future (31:17), but the travail of judgment and the reality of repentance were required for renewal. The clarity with which Jeremiah and his opponents defined and promoted opposing preceptions of the divine will should caution all persons lest they make their human judgments tantamount to divine decrees.

## Living with Trust for the Future (30:1 to 31:40)

Oracles of hope and renewal characterized Jeremiah's words beginning with the command: " 'Write in a book all the words that I have spoken to you' " (30:2). As his conflict with the prophets of Jerusalem and Babylon clarified, one facet of God's plan was judgment. Yet judgment never was—or is—God's last word; God's ultimate plans were " 'for welfare and not for evil, to give . . . a future and a hope' " (29:11). As Jeremiah later listened to Rachel weeping for her exiled children (31:15), he urged the restraint of weeping and tears on the assumption that " 'there is hope for . . . [the] future' " (31:17). In the midst of crises, the fundamental issue is God's dependability. Will he fulfill his promises, and can we trust him? Jeremiah called all persons to face crises by living with trust for the future. Such a commitment means trusting God's purposes (30:1-24) just as one trusts his love (31:1-14), his care (vv. 15-26), and his presence (vv. 27-40).

### Trusting God's Purposes (30:1-24)

The revelation of God's purposes came through oracles which Jeremiah spoke at various times during his ministry, each with positive implications for the future of Jacob (vv. 1-4). The command to write the oracles grew out of the assumption that God would restore his people's fortunes. Such motivation for writing suggests either that they were committed to writing so that they might be shared with the Exiles or that they were written to help validate Jeremiah's oracles of hope. As he told

Hananiah, when a prophet prophesied peace, only in the future would people know whether the Lord truly sent that prophet (Jer. 28:9).

God's purposes cited in chapter 30 are embedded in three prophetic oracles, each introduced by the customary, " 'Thus says the Lord' " (vv. 5,12,18). The portrait which Jeremiah sketched was one of believers trusting the Lord to free the prisoner (vv. 4-11), heal the outcast (vv. 12-17), and restore the fallen (vv. 18-24).

Freeing the prisoner (vv. 4-11) presupposes the reality of extreme need (vv. 5-9) which is counterbalanced by an appeal to fearlessness (vv. 10-11). Suffering's redemptive nature is embodied in the description of national suffering symbolized through the startling picture of a man smitten with pain often identified with childbirth (v. 6): " 'Yet he shall be saved' " (v. 7). Earlier, Jeremiah described Hananiah's unfounded action in breaking the yoke which Jeremiah wore to symbolize the captivity. Contrary to that false sign, the time would come for authentic deliverance. The Lord would " 'break the yoke from off their neck' " and would " 'burst their bonds,' " and strangers would " 'no more make servants of them' " (v. 8). God's redemptive action provided a sound basis for an appeal to Judah: " 'Fear not, O Jacob my servant, says the Lord' " (v. 10). The passage underscores the servant role of God's people.

References to Jacob and to Israel (v. 10), together with later references to Rachel's weeping (31:15), suggest that the Northern Kingdom and its exiles may have been the original context for the oracles. Yet they are set properly and firmly in the context of the Judean Exile and speak pointedly to the hope with which Jeremiah looked beyond that experience. For those bound by catastrophe, like the ancient Exiles, to trust God's purposes means to believe that he will free the prisoner. He is the true Savior who breaks the yoke and bursts the bonds (v. 8).

Healing the outcast (vv. 12-17) suggests a double malady, an incurable hurt (v. 12) and isolation as an outcast (v. 17). Here the polarizing nature of God's action emerges again in the biblical revelation. To describe the hurt as " 'incurable' " (v. 12) and to promise healing as in verse 17, or to affirm alienation as an " 'outcast . . . "for whom no one cares" ' " (v. 17) and to promise relationship, seems contradictory. Yet, today, this reminds believers that no situation rests beyond God's curative and restorative power.

God's promise is inexpressibly encouraging! Persons whose hurt was incurable, whose wound was grievous (v. 12) and for whom no medicine and no healing were available (v. 13), cried out over their hurt and pain (v. 15). How would they survive such trauma except in the Lord's grace? 'For I will restore health to you, and your wounds I will heal,' " the Lord said (v. 17) to alienated persons, whose lovers had forgotten them and cared nothing for them (v. 14). For those whom people despoiled and on whom others preyed (v. 16), outcasts for whom no one cared (v. 17), the Lord cared and would restore health. He was the One who brought such judgment (v. 15). So, the Lord would bring healing and grace to wounded persons. Today, for all persons who are wounded or alienated, the Lord still says: " 'I will restore . . . I will heal' " (v. 17). **Hope** means *waiting for the Lord to fulfill his promise.*

Renewing the nation (vv. 18-24) stresses a radically new note in Jeremiah's preaching as does chapter 30 as a whole. In his earlier oracles, he did not speak so positively of national return and renewal. Perhaps the oracles offset without minimizing the former declarations of judgment. They offered hope that was bounded only by the constraint of Judah's response. The Lord would " 'restore the fortunes of the tents of Jacob, and have compassion on his dwellings; the city . . . [would] be rebuilt upon its mound' " (v. 18). From that city would come sounds of thanksgiving; and, whereas Jeremiah earlier repudiated joy and merriment for himself, the sound of people who made merry would be heard in the restored city (v. 19).

## Trusting the Lord's Love (31:1-14)

Jeremiah believed that grace and love were the foundation stones of the Lord's faithfulness on which a joyous, worshiping community might emerge out of brokenness. Seldom does a single chapter in the Scriptures contain a more positive affirmation of love, joy, and hope to weary persons.

A love that would not let go (vv. 1-6) characterized the Lord's relationship with his people and became the foundation for new relationships. The Lord loved Israel and Judah with a love that would not let them go, for love never gives up on persons however much mature love allows persons to make their own choices. Grace would enable the people to survive disaster (v. 2), and an "everlasting love" would prompt the Lord's continued faithfulness (v. 3). Even Jeremiah's word for faithfulness (*hesed*) might be translated better as *faithful love*, for the word focused primarily on love and secondarily on faithfulness without eliminating the dynamic power of either reality. That the former blessings of the Lord were to be restored is reflected in the threefold use of " 'again' " in verses 4-5. In such a day of restoration, people again would call to each other and invite others to join a pilgrimage to Zion (v. 6). In such love manifested toward Exiles living in loneliness and isolation was the reassurance of a love that never would let go. Always, such a love rests at the heart of the divine-human relationship, and out of that love emerges a power necessary for a new quality of life:

> O love that wilt not let me go,
> I rest my weary soul in thee;
> ...............................
> That in thine ocean depths its flow
> may richer, fuller be.
> —George Matheson

The joy of a faith renewed through love (vv. 7-14) resounds throughout Jeremiah's second oracle. He was so exuberant in describing a restored people's joy that he used thirteen Hebrew words in eight verses to describe it. When faith would be renewed through love, an inexpressible joy would follow. For the Lord would save his people (v. 7) and gather them from the farthest parts of the earth (v. 8). Like a father to his son Israel, he would lead them by brooks of water (v. 9). God would keep his flock like a shepherd (v. 10) and would redeem his people from those too strong for them (v. 11). He would provide for them the goodness of the earth—grain, wine, oil, the young of the flock and the herd—so that " 'their life . . . [would be] like a watered garden' " (v. 12).

## Trusting the Lord's Care (31:15-26)

The hopelessness of the times was described under the imagery of Rachel, mother of Israel, weeping for her children (v. 15). Despite such grief, hope was offered for the future: " 'Keep your voice from weeping, and your eyes from tears; for your work shall be rewarded. . . . There is hope for your future' " (vv. 16-17). **Biblical hope** means *to wait on God*, trusting oneself to him. Either biblical hope rests on God's being there and being there for me, or it rests in another source. Yet, what source exists other than that God is real in a person's life? **"Hope"** in the Old Testament means *to wait*. Such waiting is creative, not passive as though people could contribute nothing of themselves to their situations. Yet the focus is always on what God will do.

Jeremiah described hope as integrated into human response. This is stated clearly in the characterization of Ephraim's response. Although "Ephraim" suggested the possibility of reference to the Northern Kingdom, the passage was used primarily to address the attitude which those in Exile following the destruction of Jerusalem were to manifest.

First, hope for the future exists when people recognize their rebellion: " 'I have heard Ephraim bemoaning, "Thou hast chastened me . . . like an untrained calf" ' " (v. 18). The symbol describes either obstinance or the ineptness of a calf not trained to the yoke.

Second, hope for the future is a reality when persons repent of sin and respond to correction: " ' "For after I had turned away I repented; and after I was instructed . . . I was ashamed, and I was confounded" ' " (v. 19).

Third, hope for the future is offered because of the indissoluble bond between God as father and his child: " 'Ephraim my dear son. . . . For as often as I speak against him, I do remember him still' " (v. 20). Not even the life of a prodigal closes the door on a father's memory: " 'I do remember him still' " (v. 20)!

Fourth, hope for the future is given when persons remember the way which leads back to the Lord. Jeremiah counseled Israel: " 'Set up waymarks for yourself, make yourself guideposts; consider well the highway, the road by which you went' " (v. 21).

When people embody those characteristics, they have hope for the future. Once again they can affirm this blessing in the land: " ' "The Lord bless you, O habitation of righteousness, O holy hill!" ' " (v. 23). That people could characterize Jerusalem and the precincts of the Temple as a habitation of righteousness stood in marked contrast to its former condition (7:8-12). The phrase emphasized the reformation of life produced by genuine repentance and renewal.

That Jeremiah's experience may have been conveyed through a dream is suggested by the statement: "I awoke and looked, and my sleep was pleasant to me" (v. 26). Yet the expression may have conveyed the fact that Jeremiah slept well knowing his people's condition.

## Trusting the Lord's Presence (31:27-40)

"Presence" is used to summarize this collection of Jeremiah's words which focus on the new covenant. The passage's central purpose was to affirm God's presence in the context of a new perception of relationships: " 'I will be their God, and they shall be my people' " (v. 33). In speaking of a " 'new covenant' " (v. 31), Jeremiah was like a person living on a mountain-top with clear views on either side of the mountain. In one direction, he could see in the distance the covenant made with Moses, sealed in blood and written on tablets of stone (Ex. 24:1-8). Yet having witnessed the failure of the Josianic reformation, Josiah's death, and possibly his own failure in the preaching of covenant renewal (11:1-23), Jeremiah heard a word from the Lord about new possibilities of covenant and a new basis for community.

Turning to the other side of his figurative mountain, Jeremiah viewed in the distance a " 'new covenant' " that the Lord would make with his people. The law would be within, written on their hearts as opposed to tables of stone (v. 33). Such a covenant would be internal and personal, assuring experiential knowledge of God. On such a basis, a new community could rise from the brokenness which had shattered the nation during the closing years of Jeremiah's life. Such a covenant properly highlighted God's presence in the lives of people who lived with the law in their hearts (v. 33), the knowledge of God in their midst (v. 34), and the forgiveness of sin in their consciousness (v. 34). This hope sustained Jeremiah.

Today, hope continues to sustain God's people; it is made real in the covenant ceremony of the New Testament and is repeated each time a person participates in the Lord's Supper. For in Christ, the hope of the New Covenant found its consummation: " 'This is my blood of the [new] covenant, which is poured out for many for the forgiveness of sins' " (Matt. 26:28, following the insertion of "new" as suggested by some ancient authorities).

Three ingredients were essential to the new covenant. These were individual responsibility, experiential religion, and rebuilding a holy society (vv. 27-40).

*Individual responsibility (vv. 27-30).*—Basic to implementing the new covenant and its demands was assuming personal responsibility for one's actions. People of Jeremiah's era rejected responsibility for their chaotic generation which witnessed the fall of their nation, the destruction of the Temple, and the reduction of hope to minute proportions. Believing that their situation originated not in their sins but in their fathers' sins, they quoted a proverb based in an old and widely accepted theology: the corporate solidarity of persons and the punishment for sin passed on to another generation. " ' "The fathers have eaten sour grapes, and the children's teeth are set on edge" ' " (Jer. 31:29). As an antidote to such an effort to evade guilt, Jeremiah turned the proverb against a refusal to confess guilt: " 'In those days they shall no longer say: "The fathers have eaten sour grapes, and the children's teeth are set on edge." But every one shall die for his own sin; each man who eats sour grapes, his teeth shall be set on edge' " (Jer. 31:29-30).

Each person is accountable for his or her life. Neither inherited righteousness nor inherited guilt is a part of the biblical concept of responsibility. (Compare Ezek. 18:1-32.) Apart from a strong commitment to individual responsibility, no society can endure long.

*Experiential religion* (*vv. 31-34*).—Essential for making actual a new covenant is experiential religion, for that new community can come only in the context of personal interaction with the Lord. Such a relationship is internal: The law will not appear on tables of stone as did the Decalogue but on people's hearts (v. 33). Jeremiah's conviction was much like Ezekiel's. Ezekiel expressed somewhat the same understanding:

> " 'A new heart I will give you, and a new spirit I will put within you; and I will take out of your flesh the heart of stone and give you a heart of flesh. And I will put my spirit within you, and cause you to walk in my statutes and be careful to observe my ordinances.' "
>
> —Ezekiel 36:26-27

Experiential religion focuses on personal communion with the Lord: " 'I will be their God, and they shall be my people' " (v. 33). The terms were not new, for they characterized the Old Testament concept of covenant from earlier times. Yet, old words took on new meaning when infused with the reality of experiential religion. Such communion is reflected further in the affirmation: " 'No longer shall each man teach his neighbor and each his brother, saying, "Know the Lord," for they shall

all know me' " (v. 34).

Experiential religion presupposes forgiveness: " 'For I will forgive their iniquity, and I will remember their sin no more' " (v. 34). Often a person surveys today's attitudes and wants to ask as did Karl Menninger in his book, *What ever happened to sin?* Frequently, its reality seems to be denied and its effect rationalized. Yet sin ruptures relationships—human and divine. Until a person adequately acknowledges sin's serious reality and seeks forgiveness, little possibility exists of one's implementing the covenant in life.

*Rebuilding a holy society (vv. 35-40).*—In an extended section which utilized common thought patterns and analogies of his era, Jeremiah assured the people of the reality of a new society which would emerge from the brokenness of destruction: " 'Behold, the days are coming, says the Lord, when the city shall be rebuilt for the Lord. . . . The whole valley . . . shall be sacred to the Lord' " (vv. 38,40). Unless the new covenant issues in a new conception of community while at the same time leading people to commit their lives, we well may question such a community's authenticity.

## Lessons for Life from Jeremiah 27—31

*The biblical understanding of hope as waiting on God is a model for present hope by God's people.*—Such a view places priority on God's providence. While it does not exclude individual or group initiative, it does emphasize a person's ultimate dependence on God. Believing that the issues of one's life, church, or nation are bound in God's purposes delivers one from an arrogance which assumes that self-deliverance is humanity's sole source of salvation.

*The future as the focus of hope imparts dynamic force to life's forward thrust.*—Although in nowise minimizing the present moment as the context for personal commitment, such emphasis on the future establishes hope as a reality beyond oneself. God meets individuals not only out of the past and in the present; but God comes to meet us out of the future. Christ goes before us into the future. Out of that future, God calls us to live in hope.

*The promise of a new covenant exhibits the centrality of God's promise for the future—for Jeremiah's generation, the New Testament church, and today's believers.*—That God creates new relationships is basic to humanity's hope. No word is ever God's last word, for he always has more to say to us and to do through us tomorrow than he has said or done yesterday and today. Such a new covenant became the watershed of history when the early church experienced its fulfillment through Jesus outside Jerusalem's city walls. It continues as the bond for present relationships with God and as the church's hope for the future.

---

1. William Shakespeare, *Macbeth*, act 5, scene 5, line 27.
2. W. O. Carver, *Missions in the Plan of the Ages* (Nashville: Broadman Press, 1951), p. 31.

# Personal Learning Activities

1. Jeremiah was convinced that the Exile from Jerusalem would last for _____ years.
2. Jeremiah wore _____ to symbolize Judah's impending captivity. (Choose the correct answer from the list.)
   (1) A chain       (3) A rope
   (2) A yoke       (4) A sword
3. Jeremiah counseled Zedekiah to (select the proper response from the list):
   _____(1) Resist the Babylonians
   _____(2) Surrender to the Babylonians
   _____(3) Evacuate Jerusalem
   _____(4) Trust God's deliverance
4. Match the following two lists, linking the words in the first column with the identifying phrases in the second column.
   _____(1) Hope       (a) Trusting God
   _____(2) Love       (b) The result of renewed faith
   _____(3) Faith       (c) Will not let people go
   _____(4) Joy       (d) Better translated *faithful love*
   _____(5) Faithfulness
                         (e) Waiting on God
5. Jeremiah had a marvelous vision of a new _____ for God's people.

**Answers:** 1. 70; 2. (2); 3. (2); 4. (1)e, (2)c, (3)a, (4)b, (5)d; 5. Covenant.

# 8

# Living Out of Hope

## Jeremiah 32—35

> " 'Houses and fields and vineyards shall again be bought in this land.' "—Jeremiah 32:15

Like many attitudes, confidence may be only the crystallization of people's aspirations and dreams. Trapped by experiences with which they cannot cope, many people hold desperately to confidences which prove to be groundless. Yet, the confidence which some persons have in people, institutions, and events transforms their responses to life's circumstances. In so doing, that confidence becomes a controlling factor in life. To have confidence in God and to believe his promises is to have hope, for **hope** means *to trust God*. Because **hope** means *to wait expectantly on God*, and since God had said, " 'There is hope for your future' " (31:17), the book of Jeremiah presents narratives describing what it means to live out of one's hope. These follow the prophet's oracles on hope and restoration (30—31).

Confidence in God as the controlling force of people's lives caused the optimistic hope that Jeremiah manifested in buying the family farm at Anathoth. His confidence was conceived in God (chap. 32); this led to his prophetic oracles of restoration (chap. 33). By the same token, today, to manifest less than absolute confidence in God often generates another life-style, much like that of people during crises who made agreements which they later abandoned. Their religion was one of convenience (chap. 34). Yet even confidence expressed by the Rechabites, antiquated persons of Jeremiah's era who lived by nomadic ideals, could challenge others to live with trust in the Lord. Ironically, in many ways the Rechabites had a misplaced orthodoxy (chap. 35).

## Confidence Conceived in God (32:1 to 33:26)

For Jeremiah, hope was more than a doctrinal affirmation or a troubled person's longing for better days. For him and for his successors of every generation, hope was a dynamic experience with God which gave persons an ongoing confidence. Jeremiah demonstrated that confidence through the symbolic act of buying the family farm at Anathoth, despite the fact that the seige of Jerusalem made such a purchase questionable. Jeremiah not only believed in the future, he believed in God; the two were inseparable. In examining Jeremiah's confidence which was conceived in his relationship with the Lord, the reader is confronted with a striking action in living out one's hope (32:1-44). The reader also encounters the implications for living out of one's hope (33:1-26).

### Living Out One's Hope (32:1-44)

The exhortation to "live out your faith" is a common challenge to demonstrate in life the faith which one professes. In that context, we may speak of Jeremiah's living out his hope. His action in buying the family farm at Anathoth was an object lesson and a symbolic act which affirmed his unbounded hope in the future. Because he believed in God, he also believed that houses, fields, and vineyards again would be bought in the land (v. 15). The prophet's action occurred at the most inopportune time (vv. 1-5) when a purchase seemed to be inadvisable (vv. 6-15). Indeed, Jeremiah's prayer in which he came to understand more of God's purpose emphasized that such a purchase was advisable only because of the Lord's power (vv. 16-44).

*Inopportunity of the times* (vv. 1-5).—Few purchases are less promising than a farm trampled by an invading army. Jerusalem was surrounded by the Babylonian army (v. 2), and Jeremiah was a political prisoner in the court of the guard (v. 3). Yet, he bought the family farm at Anathoth on the outskirts of the city. Anathoth was only a few miles northeast of Jerusalem and may have been occupied by the enemy. Too, because of the nature of his message, the prophet had incurred the king's dis-

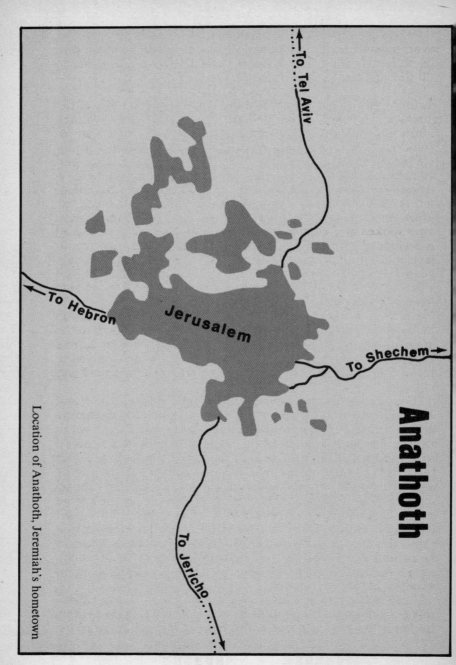

To Tel Aviv

To Hebron

Jerusalem

To Shechem

To Jericho

**Anathoth**

Location of Anathoth, Jeremiah's hometown

favor: Jerusalem would fall, and Zedekiah would be taken captive to Babylon (vv. 4-5). Against that background, the offer to sell him the family farm came to Jeremiah (vv. 6-8).

*Inadvisability of the purchase (vv. 6-15).*—Despite the inopportunity of the times and the subsequent inadvisability of the purchase, Jeremiah bought the farm as a symbol of hope in the future. In the midst of warfare, his cousin decided that he would sell the family property. Apparently, Jeremiah's family relationships were such that " ' "the right of possession and redemption" ' " (v. 8) were his. The double copy of purchase (v. 14) may have been a common business practice; more than that, in this instance, it was a way of verifying and testifying in the future of Jeremiah's confidence (v. 15). As noted before, good news spoken by prophets could be validated only by events and by written documents. Most persons living at the time would have considered the purchase inadvisable. Today, as then, only when a person believes in the future with a confidence in God is that individual able to live out his or her faith in a concrete demonstration.

*Inquiring of God (vv. 16-44).*—Jeremiah's prayer focuses on the basis for his confidence in the future and binds both to the larger purposes of God. His prayer (vv. 16-25) and the Lord's response (vv. 26-44) affirm the ground for Jeremiah's believing in the future and set the stage for the oracles of renewal and hope (33:1-26).

The prophet's prayer focuses on God's nature (vv. 16-20) and God's action (vv. 21-25). Jeremiah's praise celebrated the nature of God whose creative power demonstrated his ability to act in history. He was the Creator (v. 17) who manifested steadfast love while requiting the deeds of the guilty. According to Old Testament patterns of thought, his name summed up who he was/is: "the Lord of hosts," or armies (v. 18). He offered counsel and was mighty in deed; his eyes were open to people's ways (v. 19). Consequently, he rewarded persons in the light of their actions (v. 19). He performed wonders of redemption both in Egypt and in Jeremiah's era (v. 20). In all this, his reputation or name had been established. Jeremiah's action which manifested his confidence in the future was conceived in his understanding of God's character.

Three aspects of the Lord's action conclude the prophet's prayer. He brought his people out of Egypt (v. 21), gave to them the land "flowing with milk and honey" (vv. 22-23), and because of their disobedience brought the Babylonian crisis (v. 24). Yet God's action caused Jeremiah the greatest difficulty. Believing that the Lord caused the nation's crisis, he was puzzled concerning why the Lord had commanded him to purchase the family farm.

The Lord's response (vv. 26-44) offered a rationale for Jeremiah's purchasing the farm at Anathoth. Few would argue with the view that the times were not good or that from the human perspective the purchase was unwise. Only from the context of God does one witness the transformation of the negative and foolish into the positive and wise. The resolution of the complete issue was in God's word to Jeremiah: " 'I am the Lord, the God of all flesh; is anything too hard for me?' " (v. 27).

Growing out of God's universal, sovereign power were three oracles. Each one affirmed the wisdom of purchasing the family farm at Anathoth. The first of those oracles reaffirmed the inopportunity of the times (vv. 27-35). In the second oracle (vv. 36-41), the Lord affirmed a purpose which transcended the immediate crisis. Taking the longer look, a person often can see dawn breaking beyond darkness. So the Lord would bring the people back to the land (vv. 37-38) and would give to them singleness of heart (v. 39). He would make with them an everlasting covenant (v. 40). Then they would experience God's goodness (v. 41).

The third oracle (vv. 42-44) reaffirmed the future hope and thereby validated Jeremiah's purchasing the family farm as a symbol of confident hope in the future. " 'Fields shall be bought in this land of which you are saying, "It is a desolation" ' " (v. 43). Even when the prophet could not understand fully the reason for what he was impelled to do, he acted because of what he did know about the Lord's character.

## Living Out of One's Hope (33:1-26)

Just as Jeremiah lived out his hope by showing his confidence in the future through buying the family farm, he could live out of hope in times of crisis. Chapter 33 introduces five prophetic oracles by "thus says the Lord" or "says the Lord." Emphasis is placed on "the word of the Lord" (v. 23). These oracles clarify the ways in which hope became the reservoir out of which persons lived through captivity and Exile. Approached thematically rather than through an examination of the seven separate forms, four words epitomize what living out of hope means: restoration, rejoicing, righteousness, and reunion. Restoration is the focus running through all the emphases.

*Restoration and rejoicing (vv. 1-11).*—The restoration following the devastation of Jerusalem was described through a variety of symbols. The symbols which were used were healing and health, prosperity and security (v. 6); restoration of fortune and reconstruction of the city (v. 7); cleansing from guilt and forgiveness of sin (v. 8). Yet none of this was automatic; it was conditioned by the demand that people call to the Lord (v. 3). Such calling would find response and would result in a city of joy, praise, and glory (v. 9). People who live out of their hope believe that God will restore life from brokenness.

Joy is the outgrowth of restoration. To a land which had been waste and where streets had been desolate (v. 10), the " 'voice of mirth and the voice of gladness' " would resound again (v. 11). Jeremiah often described disaster by the loss of the kind of joy associated with marriage, just as he typified joy with the " 'voice of the bridegroom and the voice of the bride' " (v. 11). Such occasions of joy again would attend the land, and persons would sing again as they brought thank offerings to the Lord's house (v. 11).

*Restoration and righteousness (vv. 12-22).*—The oracle affirming that shepherds again would tend their sheep in the land likely had a pastoral setting when first uttered (vv. 12-13). The reference to shepherds in those verses led to the oracle which focuses on the concept of shepherd in the messianic hope (vv. 14-16; compare also vv. 17-22).

Beyond the discipline of deportation, Jeremiah saw a time when the Lord would fulfill his promise to Israel and Judah (v. 14): " 'I will cause a righteous Branch to spring forth for David' " (v. 15). A similar promise appears in 23:5-6. It builds a common prophetic hope for one like David.

The nature of the messianic reign focuses on justice and righteousness. Old Testament scholars commonly agree that the name given a person or a deity summed up some aspect of being or personality. So to note the name of this One is significant: " ' "The Lord is our righteousness" ' " (v. 16). Any discussion of the salvation of people which refuses to take seriously the attendant character of justice and righteousness is inconsistent with the biblical hope. **Righteousness** in prophetic literature meant *conformity to the relationship in which one stood with God and with other persons in the covenant.*

113

*Restoration and reunion (vv. 23-26).*—Periodically, one discovers passages in the book of Jeremiah which appear to have close ties with the kingdom of Israel and especially its renewal and the hope which this engendered. (Compare Jer. 31:1-40.) Chapter 33 closes with an affirmation of the reunion of the two nations (vv. 23-26). Other people had begun to say, " ' "The Lord has rejected the two families which he chose" ' " (v. 24), and they had despised the Lord's people (v. 24). To the contrary, affirmed the prophet, the restoration and reunion of Judah and Israel were certain.

## Convenient Religion: Contrast and Caution (34:1-22)

Chapter 34 forms a separate unit within the book of Jeremiah. This is indicated by the phrase, "The word which came to Jeremiah from the Lord" (34:1) which introduces chapter 35. The summation of chapter 34 concerns a breach of faith in which people freed their Hebrew slaves. Apparently, they freed them during a crisis situation; then they placed the slaves back in servitude. Also, chapters 32—33 focus on hope and the freeing of the Lord's people. The larger meaning of chapter 34 seems to focus on a stark contrast. The contrast was drawn between the Lord's fidelity in the promised falling and restoration of his people and Judah's faithlessness in her treatment of Hebrew slaves. Hence, the chapter is a contrast to and a caution against what might be termed "covenient religion."

### Crisis as Context (34:1-7)
The context for the present narrative rested in the seige of Jerusalem and the subjugation of the Judean cities. Jeremiah's message is well known to persons reading the book of Jeremiah: The Lord had given Jerusalem to Nebuchadrezzar (vv. 1-2), and Zedekiah would be taken captive even though he would die in peace with the goodwill of those who knew him (vv. 4-5). The Lord's word came to Jeremiah at a time when Babylon was attacking all the Judean cities and only Lachish and Azekah remained as fortified cities (vv. 7-8).

### Crisis and Covenant (34:8-10)
For whatever immediate reason, in the crisis created by the seige of Jerusalem, King Zedekiah made a covenant with the people of Jerusalem and proclaimed liberty for all Hebrew

slaves (vv. 8-9). Perhaps, the slaves were freed in order to prevent disunity in the city or to alleviate the problem of feeding the populace under seige conditions.

## Crisis and Compromise (34:11-16)

The Israelites freed the Hebrew slaves during a national crisis, "but afterward they turned around and took back the male and female slaves they had set free, and brought them into subjection as slaves" (v. 11). Why did they make this relatively sudden change of policy concerning the Hebrew slaves? Apparently, the seige had been lifted by the Egyptians' approach which caused Nebuchadrezzar's forces to shift their focus of attack. (Compare 37:5.) That the seige was lifted is stated clearly: "And Zedekiah . . . I will give into the hand of . . . [his] enemies . . . into the hand of the army of the king of Babylon which has withdrawn from you" (v. 21). Or again, "I will command, says the Lord, and will bring them [the Babylonians] back to this city" (v. 22). The picture is embarrassingly familiar and is experienced too frequently: Commitments made in a crisis soon are compromised with the passing of the crisis. To characterize such commitment as "Convenient Religion: Contrast and Caution," is not too harsh.

## Crisis and Caution (34:17-22)

Although the text does not so indicate, the narrative seems to assume that the Babylonians' removal was in response to the covenant concerning the slaves. Certainly, evidence is adequate for assuming that their return was related directly to the annulment of that covenant. (Compare vv. 11,21-22.) Because the people did not obey the Lord (v. 17), he would give to Judah a unique liberty, even as they gave and then took away another kind of liberty to the Hebrew slaves. "I proclaim to you liberty to the sword, to pestilence, and to famine" (v. 17). Continuing to caution Judah, Jeremiah said that the Lord would do to those who transgressed the covenant precisely as was done to the calf "which they cut in two and passed between its parts" (v. 18). Such a covenant ceremony was practiced in Israel during which the calf was cut in parts and the covenant parties passed between the divided sacrifice. That symbol implied a kindred fate for those who might break the bonds of the covenant so inaugurated.

**Crisis and Contrast (Compare Jer. 32—33 versus Jer. 34)**

In seeking to isolate the function of chapter 34 we suggested that it underscores the marked contrast between the Lord's fidelity (chaps. 32—33) and Judah's faithlessness (chap. 34). Although Judah maintained her commitments only so long as it was expedient, the Lord affirmed that his purpose transcended the trauma of the immediate peril.

In summary, many in Jerusalem as in every generation had what might be called a "convenient" religious commitment. When generous covenants were beneficial and expedient for them, the covenants were assumed. But when the demands of such an experience became too rigorous or the crisis passed, they dispensed quickly with the religious obligations. Such religious experiences were only for convenience.

# Contrasting Orthodoxy (35:1-19)

The orthodoxy of those nomadic idealists, the Rechabites, was unrealistic in its rejection of settled culture some 500 years after the nomadic era. But it stood in marked contrast to the shallow commitments which Judah made to the covenant. (Compare 34:1-22.) The Rechabites' orthodoxy may have been misplaced but, at least, they knew how to remain faithful to an ideal and to live out of a commitment with the power to transform life. The chapter focuses on orthodoxy demonstrated (vv. 1-11) and orthodoxy contrasted (vv. 12-19).

### Orthodoxy Demonstrated (35:1-11)

**Orthodoxy** literally means a *straight opinion* (*orthos* plus *doxa; straight* plus *opinion*) and suggests conforming to the usual beliefs or established doctrines, especially in religion. The Rechabites' demonstration of such orthodoxy became an object lesson which Jeremiah used to contrast Judah's faithlessness. The Rechabites were related to the Kenites, a seminomadic group associated with Israel since the nomadic era of the wilderness period. Their antimonarchial views were consistent with the affirmation of the desert tradition as the ideal age. Central to their conviction was the repudiation of settled life on the assumption that the wilderness and its seminomadic character was an ideal which they should continue to embody. Consequently, they refused to have vineyards or fields and lived in tents rather than villages or towns (vv.

9-10). Their presence in Jerusalem (35:1-11) was the result of Babylonian activities in the time of Jehoiakim (vv. 1,11).

Essentially, the Rechabites reacted against culture by rejecting it and by seeking to recreate the idealism of the nomadic era through living in a manner characteristic of the earlier period. In this regard, they have counterparts today who respond to modern cultural challenges by adopting the external life-style of an era long passed. These people mistakenly assume that an appropriate way to emphasize that faith is contemporary is to continue the outward characteristics of a previous era. The tragedy of this assumption is that to perpetuate a life-style is far easier than to perpetuate the faith in a new cultural setting.

Jeremiah offered the Rechabites wine to drink (vv. 2,5), knowing that they would refuse (v. 7). In doing this, he sought to communicate a positive lesson which would magnify the Rechabites' fidelity.

### Orthodoxy Contrasted (35:12-19)

Jeremiah's point was clear: Why did Judah manifest a lesser fidelity to the Lord than the Rechabites did to the traditions of Jonadab who commanded them to drink no wine (vv. 13-14)? The fault did not rest in a lack of revelation, for the Lord had sent "all . . . [his] servants the prophets . . . persistently" (v. 15). To their message of repentance, Judah turned a deaf ear. Jeremiah contrasted an orthodoxy which manifested greater fidelity to tribal ancestors than others did to the Lord (v. 16).

That orthodoxy is crucially important for God's people is obvious. Yet, the content and direction of that orthodoxy are equally crucial.

# Lessons for Life from Jeremiah 32—35

*Faith that prompts bold action during critical times emerges from the dynamic power of a personal relationship with God.*—Such a relationship has the power to transform a person's life in facing whatever life may bring. Such transformation enables an individual to face the future with confidence and boldly to confront a hazardous future in the conviction that God's larger purposes transcend immediate crises.

*Life measured solely from the human perspective may seem devoid of promise.*—Fewer purchases show less promise than a family farm in territory occupied by a national enemy. Yet, living out of his hope prompted Jeremiah to act courageously in buying the family property at Anathoth. He did so because of his unshakable conviction that God does not abandon his people.

*Standing in marked contrast to a faith which enables a person to face the future with hope is a religious experience marked by compromise.*—Jeremiah's word of caution is appropriate for anyone tempted to compromise faith and to make religious commitment a self-serving expediency.

*To all of God's people, the book of Jeremiah sounds a clear call to confront contemporary crises with hope grounded in their confidence in God's nature and action.*—All true hope rests in who God is—Creator and Redeemer.

# Personal Learning Activities

1. By purchasing the family farm in Anathoth, Jeremiah symbolized graphically _____ . (Select the proper response from the list.)
   (1) Good business judgment  (3) Utter futility
   (2) Hope for the future      (4) Wishful thinking
2. Jeremiah's action in purchasing the family farm was conceived in his understanding of _____ . (Choose the correct answer from the list.)
   (1) God's character          (3) Good investments
   (2) Family responsibilities  (4) The Babylonians' leniency
3. According to Dr. Honeycutt, four words express what *living out of hope* means. From the following list, select the four words.
   _____(1) Restoration      _____(4) Righteousness
   _____(2) Prosperity       _____(5) Comfort
   _____(3) Rejoicing        _____(6) Reunion
4. In prophetic literature, _____ meant conformity to the relationship in which a person stood with God and with other people in the covenant. (Choose the proper response from the list.)
   (1) Humility                 (3) Righteousness
   (2) Tolerance                (4) Meekness

# 9

# The Enduring Word

## Jeremiah 36—39

Now, after the king had burned the scroll. . . .—Jeremiah 36:27

The Bible endures through all generations, crises, and cultures. Surviving the attacks of its enemies and the protection of its friends, the written Word of God continues to generate the reality of God's presence. Despite the adversities which sometimes surround the creation, transmission, and interpretation of Scripture it mediates God's authoritative revelation. It continues to be a lively medium for God's presence generated through persons, words, and events. Scripture survived adversity and neglect, and it created the context for God's meeting persons through the power of the enduring Word. The Word of God is more than words; should a person destroy the words of a scroll as Jehoiakim did (36:23-25), the Word endures as God's creative presence. Through such a Word, Jeremiah was inspired to write the scroll again. He added to it other words that were not included in the first scroll which Jehoiakim had destroyed. (Compare 36:28,32.)

The chapters which are introduced by the phrase, "This Word came to Jeremiah from the Lord" (36:1), may be summarized thematically by considering the indestructible Word (36:1-32) and the fulfilled Word (37:1 to 39:18). The former theme focuses on the writing of Jeremiah's oracles and Jehoiakim's attempt to destroy them. The latter empahsizes the way in which the Word was fulfilled in history.

# The Indestructible Word (36:1-32)

Persons may destroy the words which form Scripture, but they cannot destroy the Word of God. Such a Word is synonymous with God's creative power experienced in history. Consistently, the Word in Jeremiah is introduced by a verb of being (*hayah, to be*) and might be translated: *The Word of the Lord happened* or *occurred*. God's creative sharing of himself is not subject to human intervention or suspension. Yet, the Word seeks words as a medium for sharing God's revelation. For this reason, the Lord commanded Jeremiah to rewrite the words that he had spoken through the prophet (v. 2). In the process of putting his spoken words into written form (vv. 1-8), Jeremiah communicated the words with others (vv. 9-26); in rewriting the scroll, he demonstrated the continuity between word and revelation (vv. 27-32).

## Committing Experiences to Words (vv. 1-8)

The Bible is the record of God's revelation through inspired persons who recorded events and interpreted them in faith in God. Yet, the Bible is far more than a record of past revelation. Through the power of God's Spirit, it can become the medium for the contemporary revelation of God. This seems to have been the primary purpose in the Lord's command that Jeremiah write the words which he had spoken during the almost twenty years since his ministry began in the time of Josiah (vv. 1-3).

*The inspiration of Scripture (vv. 1-3).*—Inspiration is presupposed in the Bible: "All scripture is inspired by God" (2 Tim. 3:16). The command that Jeremiah write the oracles spoken since the beginning of his ministry during the fifth year of Josiah, almost twenty years earlier, suggests that he wrote at God's initiative: "This word came to Jeremiah from the Lord" (v. 1). The original oracle and the recollection and transcription of the material to written form were inspired.

*The process of writing Scripture (vv. 4-8).*—Jeremiah used Baruch as a "secretary" (36:26) to whom he dictated those oracles spoken against Israel, Judah, and the nations since the beginning of the prophet's ministry under Josiah (v. 2; compare 4,17-19). Since the command to write came in the "fourth year of Jehoiakim" (v. 1), and the scroll was read to the people in the ninth month of the fifth year (v. 9), writing the oracles may have required a lengthy period of time.

The process of writing the scroll reflects at least two factors commonly associated with writing Scripture. First, the writing of the oracles arose in a context of need. Jehoiakim's poor performance as successor to good King Josiah, the emergence of the Babylonian crisis, and the need for covenant renewal among God's people were some of the factors which called for the reproduction of Jeremiah's oracles. By Jeremiah's reproducing those oracles, people of another day could experience God's revelation. Also, Jeremiah had been " 'debarred from going to the house of the Lord' " (v. 5); therefore, the oracles may have been written in order to permit the prophet's message to be communicated by Baruch on Jeremiah's behalf. Furthermore, to write the spoken oracles may have intensified their authority and power. Baruch's standing in the Temple and reading the oracles of doom constituted a symbolic act. The oracles were fraught with the power of the symbolic act. Jeremiah committed the oracles to written form in order to meet human needs.

Second, the writing of the oracles (and Scripture generally) had redemptive intent. The purpose for writing the oracles is stated clearly: " 'It may be that the house of Judah will hear . . . so that every one may turn . . . and that I may forgive their iniquity and their sin' " (v. 3). The Bible is concerned with what we might term "salvation history." Scripture came from faith to faith in that it proceeded from a perspective of faith commitment and was intended to lead to a comparable commitment in faith to the Lord.

## Communicating the Words of Revelation (36:9-26)

God intended that Scripture and the revelation which it generates are to be shared. That this was so of the oracles which Jeremiah dictated to Baruch is evidenced by the fact that the scroll was dictated for the specific purpose of being read to the people in the Temple (v. 6). Within the bounds of revelation created through the prophet's written words, three concentric circles of hearers were included: the people (vv. 9-10), the princes of the land (vv. 11-19), and the king (vv. 20-26).

*Hearing the words (vv. 9-10).*—A minimum of nine months separated the command to write the oracles and the reading of the words in the Temple. (Compare vv. 1,9.) People of Jerusalem and the cities of Judah had gathered for a fast at the Temple (v. 9). In such a setting, Baruch read the scroll containing Jeremiah's words (v. 10). Fasts often accompanied times of

121

national lamentation because of a major crisis. The fast in verse 9 may have been related to the attacks against Jerusalem after Jehoiakim's rebellion following three years of loyalty to Nebuchadnezzar. Should this have been the case, the intense hostility caused by Jeremiah's oracles of doom becomes more understandable.

*Responding to the words (vv. 11-19).*—Among those in the Temple who heard Baruch read the scroll was Micaiah (v. 11) who immediately reported to the princes of the land the words that he had heard (vv. 12-13). Apparently, the princes desired to hear for themselves the doom oracles, so they sent for Baruch to bring the scroll to them in the king's house (v. 14). They responded in fear to the doom oracles (v. 16); the fact that they felt obliged to report the scroll to the king, plus their counsel that Baruch and Jeremiah hide (v. 19), suggest that an ominous context was created by the reading of the words.

Again, the fact that the scroll was read on a fast day strongly suggests a day of national lamentation. If such a lamentation was related to the crisis generated by the Babylonians and their allies marshalled against Judah, then the gravity of the princes' response falls into perspective. Yet, whatever the princes' motivation, the scroll's content was enough to require that it be reported to the king. Also, their concern for the prophet led them to counsel Baruch and Jeremiah to hide (v. 19).

*Destroying the words (vv. 20-26).*—The scroll was read in early winter, "the ninth month," and King Jehoiakim "was sitting in the winter house and there was a fire burning in the brazier" (v. 22). As Jehudi read three or four columns of the scroll, the king cut them off with a penknife and threw them into the fire (v. 23). That the king was unimpressed with Jeremiah's words was reflected not only in his destruction of the scroll but also in the observation that "neither the king, or any of his servants who heard all these words, was afraid" (v. 24).

## Continuity of Word and Revelation (36:27-32)

Not even the malicious action of a despotic king brought an end to God's revelation. Continuity between word and revelation assures that revelation can generate additional words. Stated otherwise, God's revelation is not bound to the particular words of a given situation. After the burning of the scroll, the Word came to Jeremiah again. He was commanded to take a second scroll and to dictate the words which were on the first scroll. To this he added the admonition directed to Jehoiakim (vv. 29-31); and, when the scroll was rewritten, "many similiar words were added to them" (v. 32).

So, the Word's indestructible character emerged in the prophetic and kingly conflict over the writing of what later was accepted as canonical Scripture. Yet, Scripture does not need human defense nearly as much as it needs interpretation and proclamation. God is able to care for his Word, however much he may use human personality. As the Lord said to Jeremiah, " 'I am watching over my word to perform it' " (1:12).

## The Fulfilled Word (37:1 to 39:18)

The Word that has been indestructible in history also has been fulfilled through history. Such fulfillment was apparent in the interviews of Jeremiah and Zedekiah (chaps. 37—38) and in the destruction of Jerusalem by the Babylonian assault (chap. 39). Here, originally separate and distinct materials develop a consistent theological motif. For example, the first chapter of the larger unit (chaps. 36—39) was from the fourth year of Jehoiakim (36:1). The interviews of Zedekiah and Jeremiah (chaps. 37—38) occurred during the seige of Jerusalem and the withdrawal of the Babylonians when confronted by the Egyptians in the time of Zedekiah (37:1-5). The account of Jerusalem's seige and capture essentially is the same narrative recorded in the book of Kings. (Compare 2 Kings 25:1-7.) What was the writer's purpose in taking material from three periods of time and combining them under the introductory statement, "This word came to Jeremiah from the Lord" (36:1)? Apparently, the purpose was to show the theological continuity between the enduring word and historical events, especially the manner in which history was the forum for that fulfillment.

### Faithful Prophet and Fearful King (37:1 to 38:28)

Zedekiah's developing character captivates a person's attention as it unfolds in the book of Jeremiah. Obviously a person who sought God's will, he apparently developed neither the resolve nor the determination necessary to implement that will. Consequently, according to various narratives, he sought the prophet's counsel or invited his prayer. Then he ignored coun-

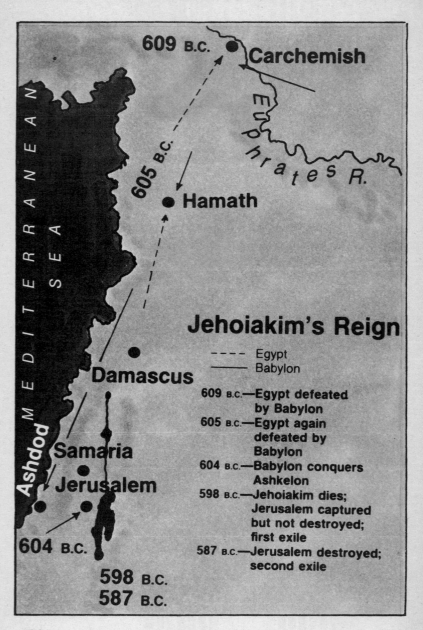

609 B.C. Carchemish

*Euphrates R.*

605 B.C.

Hamath

MEDITERRANEAN SEA

Damascus

Ashdod

Samaria

Jerusalem

604 B.C.

598 B.C.
587 B.C.

## Jehoiakim's Reign

- - - - Egypt
——— Babylon

609 B.C.—Egypt defeated
by Babylon
605 B.C.—Egypt again
defeated by
Babylon
604 B.C.—Babylon conquers
Ashkelon
598 B.C.—Jehoiakim dies;
Jerusalem captured
but not destroyed;
first exile
587 B.C.—Jerusalem destroyed;
second exile

sel and thwarted prayer. He seemed sympathetic with Jeremiah, for he offered the prophet protection, even when Jeremiah spoke of the city's doom and the king's deportation. Jeremiah was both counselor (chap. 37) and confidant (chap. 38) to the king but with little alteration of Zedekiah's conduct. Zedekiah impresses the reader as neither a malicious man like Jehoiakim nor as a coward like Jehoiachin. Yet he was fundamentally a weak, fearful man.

*Seek a prophetic word* (37:1-21).—People need a word from beyond themselves when they live in chaotic times like those of Zedekiah, the covenant nation's last king. In such a crisis, we should not be surprised that Zedekiah called for Jeremiah and asked whether he had " 'any word from the Lord' " (vv. 16-21). Now as then, in response to such a quest for the Word beyond all other words, chapter 38 speaks most pointedly.

Jeremiah proclaimed the Lord's word and announced Zedekiah's ultimate defeat (vv. 1-10). Consistent with other messages of doom, Jeremiah identified the cause for Zedekiah's downfall as his consistent refusal to obey (hear or listen to) the "words of the Lord" (v. 2). In such a context, Zedekiah asked Jeremiah: " 'Pray for us to the Lord our God' " (v. 3). Yet Jeremiah's response was not to pray but to reiterate the word of doom and to insist that the Babylonians' withdrawal, because of Egyptian pressure, was only a temporary relief (v. 5).

The Lord's prophet was accused falsely. The princes of Judah accused Jeremiah of treason (vv. 11-15). The context for such an accusation was the Chaldean (Babylonian) army's temporary withdrawal from Jerusalem at the Egyptians' approach (v. 11). Having bought the family farm at Anathoth during his forced seclusion in the court of the guard (32:1-15), "Jeremiah set out from Jerusalem to go to the land of Benjamin to receive his portion there among the people" (v. 12). Accosted by the sentry (v. 13), Jeremiah was accused of desertion and carried to the princes who beat him and imprisoned him in the house of Jonathan the secretary (v. 15).

Seeking the Lord's revelation, Zedekiah sent for Jeremiah where he was lodged in the "dungeon cells" (v. 16) and asked what has become a classic question: " 'Is there any word from the Lord?' " (v. 17). The king sought God's revelation in a time of crisis; but Zedekiah already had received Jeremiah's declarations of that Word to which the king would not listen! Like so many people what Zedekiah probably sought was some other word, a word of hope and assurance. Again, Jeremiah reiterated his word of doom. Yet even in the announcement of disaster, the friendship of king for prophet emerged. For if they were enemies, Jeremiah and Zedekiah were friendly enemies. Jeremiah asked that he not be returned to the dungeon cells of Jonathan's house lest he die there (v. 20). Zedekiah granted his request.

*Confiding in a prophet (38:1-28).*—The friendship of the prophet and the king appeared again in chapter 38 as the king delivered Jeremiah from an ominous fate (vv. 7-13). Later, he sent for Jeremiah to share the confidences of a beleaguered sovereign (vv. 14-27). As the lengthening shadows of disaster spread across the city, Zedekiah's agony and distress grew darker. Where could he turn, if not to his friendly enemy the prophet who shared God's word with integrity?

Misunderstanding the Lord's prophet, those who heard him accused Jeremiah of treason (38:1-7). For Jeremiah to function as both critic and supporter of the institution was not easy. Although he believed that Judah would not surrender to the Babylonians and thereby save the city, he continued to counsel surrender. Needless to say, such a message during the seige was open not only to suspicion but to direct charges of treason. This sprang from the further elaboration of Jeremiah's message. Whereas he had advised surrender of the city, he began to counsel defection by individuals (vv. 2-3). The princes' counsel to the king was clear: " 'Let this man be put to death, for he is weakening the hands of the soldiers who are left in this city. . . . For this man is not seeking the welfare of this people, but their harm' " (v. 4). In the face of such logic, the king was left with no recourse other than agreement.

The Lord's prophet was rescued when the king supported Ebedmelech (vv. 7-14). The princes had intended to kill Jeremiah by letting him starve in the waterless cistern into which they had cast him. (Compare vv. 4,9.) Even when Jeremiah's condemnation by the princes precluded Zedekiah's public support, he helped in delivering his friend and formal enemy, God's prophet.

Confiding in the Lord's prophet, Zedekiah continued to affirm Jeremiah (vv. 14-28). How would you assess the foundation of the relationship between the king and the prophet? Clearly their relationship was founded on total *honesty*. This was reflected in Zedekiah's statement, " 'I will ask you a question; hide nothing from me' " (v. 14). Jeremiah feared that the king might take his life should he speak the truth of God's message; however, the king assured him, " 'I will not put you to death' " (v. 16). Authentic relationships can exist only when persons are mutually committed to complete integrity.

Jeremiah and Zedekiah's relationship was marked by a commitment to confidences (vv. 24-28). Zedekiah was fearful that the princes would come to Jeremiah and seek to determine the nature of their conversation. The king told Jeremiah to say that the prophet had made " ' "a humble plea to the king that he would not send . . . [him] back to the house of Jonathan to die there" ' " (v. 26). The princes did come to ask about Jeremiah's conversation with the king, and Jeremiah "answered them as the king had instructed him" (v. 27).

## Fulfilling the Lord's Word Through History (39:1-18)

For all practical purposes, chapter 39 is identical to 2 Kings 25:1-7. It affirms that the Lord's Word endures and, that in so doing, it is fulfilled through history. Israel's view of history affirmed that God stood at the center of history and that all history should be evaluated from the perspective of the centrality of God. Such a theocentric view of history led to theocracy as a form of government and to a view of last things which affirmed that God would be as triumphant in the end as he was in the beginning. Although the fall of Jerusalem was by no means the end of history, it affirmed the focus of history as revelatory of God's purpose. It also focused more clearly on the reality of God as the One who stands at the center of history as well as at the end.

*The fate of Zedekiah and the destruction of Jerusalem (vv. 1-10).*—The books of Jeremiah and 2 Kings agree that the seige lasted eighteen months. The Kings narrative suggests that the famine was so severe (2 Kings 25:3) that a breach was made in the wall through which the king and the men of war fled by night (v. 4). The book of Jeremiah agrees with the date of the breach in the wall but adds: "When Jerusalem was taken, all the princes of the king of Babylon came and sat in the middle gate. . . . When Zedekiah king of Judah and all the soldiers saw them, they fled, going out of the city at night" (vv. 3-4).

Zedekiah's fate was particularly sad, for he was captured on the plains of Jericho (v. 5); the Babylonians carried him to Nebuchadrezzar at Riblah, in the land of Hamath to the north of

Israel (v. 5). There the king passed judgment on Zedekiah. He slew Zedekiah's sons before Zedekiah's eyes were put out, condemning him to live all his days with the sight of the sons whom he had failed and the blood that he had spilled.

Between three and four weeks afterward, Jerusalem was devastated. The king's house was burned as were the people's houses, and the Babylonians broke down the city walls (v. 8). The book of Jeremiah makes no reference at this juncture to the Temple, although the book of Kings indicates that it, too, was burned. (Compare 52:13; 2 Kings 25:9.) Apparently the total population was not deported, for Jeremiah mentioned "the poor" left in the land to whom were given vineyards and fields at the time of the destruction (v. 10). Apparently, the primary leaders were deported.

*The future of Jeremiah* (*vv. 11-14*).—Jeremiah's positive fate stood in marked contrast to the awesome judgment on Zedekiah. The prophet received consideration from Nebuchadrezzar through Nebuzaradan, the captain of the guard who arrived in Jerusalem approximately a month after the king's flight. The command to care for Jeremiah was all-inclusive: " 'Take him, look after him well and do him no harm, but deal with him as he tells you' " (v. 12). Fulfilling this command, the Babylonian officers entrusted the prophet to the care of Gedaliah the son of Ahikam, son of Shaphan (v. 14).

*The fidelity of Ebed-melech* (*vv. 15-18*).—Ebed-melech, whose name described his function as servant of the king, was an Ethiopian who had delivered Jeremiah when the prophet was condemned to death for treason (38:7-13). While Jeremiah was imprisoned, the Lord spoke to him concerning the deliverance of Ebed-melech when Jerusalem was destroyed.

In retrospect, history validated the Word that came to Jeremiah. The Lord's Word triumphed over both the malignant evil epitomized in kings like Jehoiakim and the careless, indifferent persons like those living during the last days of Jerusalem.

## Lessons for Life from Jeremiah 36—39

*The indestructible character of God's Word rests in its equation with God's creative, redeeming presence.*—Word is always more than merely words, however much words become the primary vehicle for creating the dynamic experience of God as Word. In a generation which is addicted to a disposable mentality and which values too lightly enduring objects and qualities, what remains? With prophets and apostles, a person can affirm that the Word of our God endures forever.

*The dynamic nature of the Scriptures' formation, clearly illustrated in the events surrounding Jehoiakim's malicious effort to destroy the scroll of Jeremiah, emphasizes the role of God's Spirit.* God's Spirit guided those who wrote the Bible just as he guides those who interpret the Scriptures.

Real freedom never is license to do whatever one wants. Persons respond to the Bible under the leadership of the Holy Spirit who was present in the Bible's creation and who overshadowed its growth and preservation. Today, he continues as the necessary Person in the interpretation of the Scriptures.

*We experience God's enduring Word in history.*—The historical detail of Jeremiah 37—39 affirms that history is the arena where an individual meets the Word. In the flow of actual events and personalities, God's Word happens. It is always a happening, an event, or an experience.

# Personal Learning Activities

1. According to Dr. Honeycutt, Scripture needs defense more than it needs interpretation and proclamation. True _____ False _____
2. Jeremiah was counselor and confidant to King _____ . (Choose the correct answer from the list.)
   (1) Zedekiah       (3) Josiah
   (2) Jehoiakim       (4) Jehoiachin
3. Jeremiah's message urging surrender to the Babylonians was open to the charge of (choose the correct response from the list):
   _____(1) Blasphemy       (3) Poor counsel
   _____(2) Error       (4) Treason
4. Jeremiah was rescued by _____ . (Select the proper response from the list.)
   (1) Baruch       (3) Ebed-melech
   (2) Jehudi       (4) Jehoiakim

**Answers:** 1. False; 2. (1); 3. (4); 4. (3).

Breach in wall of Jerusalem
130

# 10

# And What of the Future?

## Jeremiah 40—52

"Pray . . . that the Lord your God may show us the way we should go, and the thing we should do."—Jeremiah 42:2-3

Life so often is much like the children's nursery rhyme of that egg-shaped figure, Humpty Dumpty:

Humpty Dumpty sat on a wall,
    Humpty Dumpty had a great fall.
    All the king's horses,
    All the king's men,
Couldn't put Humpty together again.[1]

As the cartoon illustrating that rhyme so vividly suggests through the sketches of the egg-shaped Humpty Dumpty, sometimes life's brokenness is like an egg smashing on the ground. Though a person tries desperately, life cannot seem to be put together again, not like it once was.

When such occasions come in people's lives, many respond by longing for another opportunity. To the remnant left in Judah during the Exile, such an opportunity came for them to begin again. To be sure, life could not be started over as it had been. Life never could be precisely as it once was. Everywhere were the vestiges of war and conquest. Today, life never can be exactly the same again as an individual seeks the opportunity for a new beginning. Yet it can be rebuilt on different foundations. This was the opportunity which Judeans faced following the destruction of the Temple.

Who would God's people be and what would be their relationship with the Lord and with other persons in the richness of covenant living? Jeremiah's fidelity to the Lord as well as the truth of his word had been validated by Jerusalem's destruction and the Exile of which he had forewarned Judah. Leaders largely responsible for the disgrace of defeat and the disintegration of religious structures had been carried into Exile. Left to their successors as leaders of a remnant people was the opportunity of a new beginning. Jeremiah not only survived the city's destruction but did so with the Babylonians' good favor, and he was well received by the remnant under the governor, Gedaliah. God's purposes for fulfilling the covenant hope were as authentic as ever. Through the prophet, he had assured his people of a future.

The chapters in Jeremiah which follow the description of Jerusalem's fall (compare 39:1-17) focus on the way that the remnant responded to life following the end of the nation. The diverse material consists of narratives that describe events immediately after Jerusalem's fall (chaps. 40—45), an extended section of oracles against the nations (chaps. 46—51), and an historical review almost identical to 2 Kings 24:18 to 25:30. By linking in the larger context these three types of material which are so different in literary form and date, the writer interpreted life by the remnant as basically a reliving of yesterday's errors (chaps. 40—45). He emphasized the wisdom of committing life to God's sovereign power, much as in ancient "holy war" (chaps. 46—51). Use of historical material reaffirmed the validity of Jeremiah's prophetic mission (chap. 52).

## Reliving Yesterday's Errors (40:1 to 45:5)

Even when people receive the gift of a new opportunity, the future will be no better than the past unless they are different. Not chronology, but the commitments of life assure the renewal of a society. More than another chance, people need new hearts; and more than that, they need new spirits.

One turns to the new phase in the remnant's life with the conviction that surely they would heed the prophet's words and follow the Lord's will. Yet, failure followed failure (chaps. 40—45) until the remnant merely was reliving former errors. Only through an intensive period of refinement such as emerged in Exilic and post-Exilic Judaism could come the new heart and the new spirit of which prophets spoke.

## When the End Comes (40:1 to 43:13)

Despite the utopian hopes for the future which followed the city's destruction, the remnant reflected a diverse composition determined by the nature of human responses. For some, this period was one of grace and mercy mingled with the opportunity of a new beginning. Others responded with no more sensitivity than those responsible for the city's fall. Still others learned little from the debacle of Jerusalem's destruction; thus, they continued their infidelity and changed only the locale of their apostasy from Judah to Egypt. Chapters 40—43 focus on the observation that judgment fell with mercy for some (40:1-16), was unheeded by others (41:1-17), came with prophetic warning of repetition (42:1 to 43:7), and had inexorable power that reached even to Egypt (43:8-13).

*The end comes with mercy (40:1-16).*—For Jeremiah and the people, the end of the nation was not without mercy. Jeremiah's fate (vv. 1-6) was most gracious. Probably this consideration was the direct result of his efforts to convince Zedekiah that a policy of surrender was to Judah's long-term benefit. Although Jeremiah was taken in chains with other captives to Ramah (v. 1), Nebuzaradan freed him and offered him the choice of going to Babylon or remaining in the land (v. 4). Should he remain, he was to return to Gedaliah, governor of the cities of Judah who dwelt at Mizpah (vv. 5-6). The people's future seemed promising as Gedaliah provided leadership for an enlarging number of persons (vv. 7-12).

In addition to those already associated with Gedaliah at Mizpah, two groups constituted the basis for growth. Bands of "forces" dispersed by the Babylonian assault made their way to Gedaliah (vv. 7-9) as well as "Jews" who were living in Moab, Ammon, and Edom (vv. 11-12). To all, Gedaliah gave essentially the same advice that Jeremiah had provided in his letter to the Exiles (compare 29:1-9): " 'Do not be afraid to serve the Chaldeans. Dwell in the land, and serve the king of Babylon, and it shall be well with you' " (40:9).

Based on the return of various groups to Gedaliah and his counsel to the returnees, the possibility of learning from Jerusalem's sad experience and the opportunity of building a new community were viable options. Life apparently progressed well in the early, regrouping stages which followed Jerusalem's destruction. Yet, the people's failure to recognize evil for what it was sounded the end for the new community

(vv. 13-16). Johanan, one of the leaders of the forces in the open country, came to Gedaliah to warn him that Ishmael was a tool of the Ammonites. Ishmael had come to Mizpah not to join forces with Gedaliah but to kill him (vv. 13-14).

Gedaliah's defense of Ishmael and his refusal to support his removal resulted in Gedaliah's death and the scattering of the new community.

*The end comes unheeded (41:1-18).*—Why do people refuse to learn from history? They seem driven to learn everything solely through personal experiences. Rebellion against the Babylonians had ended the nation of Judah and its religious and cultural phenomena. Yet no sooner than the refugees had begun to develop a new community, forces of disruption emerged. Those forces functioned precisely as others before them who had caused the city's fall. The end of the nation came unheeded for them.

Ishmael's uprising (vv. 1-10) resulted in the death of Gedaliah, all the Jews who were with him at Mizpah, and the Chaldean soldiers who happened to be there (vv. 2-3). Following that, eighty men came from Shechem with gifts to offer at the Temple. Ishmael met them, invited them to see Gedaliah, and then slew seventy of the worshipers (vv. 4-7).

Johanan's defeat of Ishmael (vv. 11-18) was followed by flight to Egypt. Johanan was the one who had warned Gedaliah about Ishmael's plot (40:13-15), and he had pursued Ishmael and brought back the captives from Gibeon. The damage which Ishmael had done could not be rectified, especially his slaughter of Gedaliah whom the Babylonians had appointed as governor. Consequently, Johanan and his group settled temporarily near Bethlehem with the intention of going to Egypt (v. 17). The narrative sounds like a replay of earlier events which Jeremiah confronted; the people appeared to have learned little from the experiences associated with Jerusalem's fall. For them, the end came unheeded.

*The end comes with prophetic warning (42:1 to 43:7).*—The people's inquiring of Jeremiah (vv. 1-6) left the impression that nothing was done without consulting the prophet about God's purposes. Johanan's request for prayer was appropriate: " 'Pray . . . for all this remnant . . . that the Lord your God may show us the way we should go, and the thing we should do' " (vv. 2-3). In response to the prophet's assurance that he would pray and keep back nothing that the Lord might reveal to him, Johanan committed the people to do according to all the word which the Lord would send (v. 5).

The Lord's response (vv. 7-22) did not support the remnant's desires. Jeremiah said: If you remain in the land, accept Babylonian sovereignty and rebuild your society; and the Lord will be with you (vv. 7-17). On the other hand, should they flee into Egypt they would experience the same fate as those who inhabited Jerusalem and witnessed its downfall (vv. 18-22).

The remnant's reaction (43:1-7) underscored their determination to go into Egypt. They failed to receive from the prophet a response consistent with their position. They accused him of lying (v. 2) and of being part of a plot to hand them over to the Babylonians (v. 3). Johanan and his followers rejected the Lord's counsel and fled into Egypt (vv. 6-7). Their action underscored their folly of agreeing to abide by an unknown decision (42:5-6) and the hypocrisy of following the Lord only when his will was consistent with their desires.

*The end comes with inescapable power (43:8-13)*.—Shifting the arena of encounter from Judah to Egypt did not eliminate the Lord's power to act in history! God's revelation came as clearly in one country as in another: "The word of the Lord came to Jeremiah in Taphanhēs" (v. 8). Jeremiah communicated that revelation by symbolic action which was as effective in Egypt as it was in Judah (vv. 9-13). Taking large stones, he hid them in the mortar of the pavement at the entrance to Pharaoh's palace in Taphahnēs (v. 9). Then he warned the remnant that the Lord would send Nebuchadnezzar who would set this throne above those stones before the Pharaoh's palace (v. 10). The Babylonians would smite Egypt with pestilence, sword, and captivity (v. 11). Burning the temples and carrying away captives, Nebuchadnezzar would " 'clean the land of Egypt, as a shepherd cleans his cloak of vermin' " (v. 12). No way was available to escape such universal power. Judah was left with no option other than to live with that quality of life which was able to pass safely through the fires of testing and refining. Renewal of life, not escape, remained an appropriate response to the Lord's inescapable power.

## When Persons Will Not Learn (44:1-30)

Fundamental to the rationale for Judah's destruction was national apostasy. Especially was the worship of a foreign deity such as the "queen of heaven" integral to that apostasy. (Compare 7:16-20.) Normally, people tend to learn from their mistakes and will not repeat the same misadventure. Not so with the remnant! No sooner had they settled in Egypt than they initiated an apostasy closely related to that which had brought Jerusalem's judgment. Jeremiah cautioned these people who practiced apostasy by worshiping the gods of Egypt (vv. 1-14). Throughout the chapter, his primary thesis was that the remnant was doing precisely what brought about Jerusalem's fall.

A spirit of contempt for the prophet characterized the people's rejection of his counsel (vv. 15-19). Their rejection was direct: " 'As for the word which you have spoken to us in the name of the Lord, we will not listen to you' " (v. 16). Apparently, the remnant was convinced that worshiping the queen of heaven brought prosperity and that only when they had ceased such worship had difficult times emerged (vv. 17-19).

Jeremiah's rebuttal of the remnant was a challenge to trial by history (vv. 20-30). Not only should the remnant remember the historical cause for Jerusalem's fall, they would know whether their word or the prophet's word was valid by a sign that the prophet gave. " 'This shall be the sign to you. . . . Behold, I will give Pharaoh Hophra king of Egypt . . . into the hand of those who seek his life' " (vv. 29-30). That the remnant refused to learn from history is obvious in the biblical record.

### When All Is Lost (45:1-5)

Chapter 45 originally was located with the oracles that Jeremiah dictated to Baruch in the fourth year of Jehoiakim (v. 2; compare 36:1-3). The oracle reflected the sorrow and weariness that Baruch experienced during the conflict with Jehoiakim (v. 3). It also reflected a promise: Despite the fact that the Lord was destroying the land (v. 4), he would remember Baruch and deliver him out of the crisis (v. 5).

This oracle, placed in the context of the Egyptian crisis, effectively sounded the last note for those hoping to be delivered by association with Egypt. Such usage excellently illustrated the way in which the prophet wrote an oracle for one use and then placed it within the canon to give it a new function in a different context. Once the oracle might have been used to sound the death knell for Judah; so later, it was used to affirm that all was lost for the remnant in Egypt. With this emphasis, the narratives (chaps. 40—45) have run full cycle, following the same pattern as those concerning the nation. Given the opportunity of developing a new community in which persons lived out of their relationships with God and with one another in the covenant, Judah and the remnant choose another way.

## Committing Life to God's Sovereign Power
## (46:1 to 51:64)

The oracles against foreign nations (chaps. 46—51) affirm the Lord's sovereign power in the affairs of nations. Modeled after the concept of holy war, they portray the Lord as the warrior God who fought his people's battles. Such oracles of triumph and victory logically were to be associated with the future hope of God's people. From one perspective, they spoke of the Old Testament writers' larger eschatological goal. This goal will be achieved when the Day of the Lord has reached fruition and the kingdoms of this earth have become the kingdom of our Lord through the processes of history. A summary attempt toward understanding the oracles must be made: They should be set in their larger context in prophetic literature.

The significance of the oracles against foreign nations for prophetic literature is indicated by their appearance in each of the major prophets: Isaiah (chaps. 13—23), Jeremiah (chaps. 46—51), and Ezekiel (chaps. 25—32). Furthermore, in Jeremiah, the oracles against Egypt, the Philistines, Moab, Ammon, Edom, Damascus, Kedar/Hazor, Elam, and Babylon occupy about 10 percent of the total book. A literary form that was used so consistently by major prophets obviously played a unique role in Old Testament theology.

That the oracles fulfilled a function unique in themselves is suggested by the fact that they were placed following Jeremiah, chapter 25 in the Septuagint (the Greek translation of the Old Testament). In the Hebrew text, they were placed following the narratives on the remnant's fate. Apparently the oracles fulfilled so unique a collective function that they were used in more than a single place in the text. Stated otherwise, their meaning grew out of their content more than it grew out of the larger context.

The oracles against foreign nations reflected the ideology of the holy war associated with the conquest; however, much of that ideology may have been reshaped for a different cultural era. As such, the oracles affirmed that the victories achieved in the conquest would be repeated as the Lord returned as a warrior God to vanquish those who opposed his kingdom. Conceptually, many aspects of the oracles have moved beyond the ideology of holy war. An example is the developed emphasis on the use of other nations in history as the forum for the Lord's victory. Yet the concept of the Lord as the warrior who leads his people to victory remains, regardless of his standing behind the conquering nations rather than in the forefront as a divine warrior leading Israel.

As stated previously, the oracles reflected an eschatological connotation within each of the several contexts. In Jeremiah, the Hebrew text placed them immediately after the misfortunes of the remnant in Egypt. Isaiah located the foreign oracles immediately prior to the commonly designated apocalyptic section (Isa. 24—27). Ezekiel located the oracles against the nations in an order which suggests that they were preparatory to the great work of restoring God's people. (Compare chaps. 33—39.) In Jeremiah, for example, such a day of triumph was described as "the day of the Lord," a common eschatological phrase presupposed as early as Amos. (Compare Amos 5:18.)

The oracles against foreign nations consistently utilized highly poetic language and an exalted imagery to describe the triumph of God's people through their enemies' defeat. The texts should be exegeted with sensitivity, in a poetic mood, and with an awareness of the extensive use of imagery.

The oracles were not so much the products of despair as they were dreams of victory in times of great oppression and crisis. As such they were related to emerging apocalyptic literature which pointed to God's triumph in history.

We must try to understand why the oracles appear as they do following the narrative on the remnant (Jer. 40—45). Especially, we must attempt to assess their theological function in the text of Jeremiah. In the context of the remnant's failure which came through their theological rebellion and their being ravished by the nations, the oracles against the nations affirmed God's ultimate triumph in history. As such, they encouraged the people of the remnant to commit their lives to the Lord who is sovereign in history. Israel and Judah may have failed while the nations of their historical era appeared to prosper, but the last word was always God's.

The oracles against the nations are contained in the following blocks of Scripture:

Egypt (46:1-28)

Philistines (47:1-7)
Moab (48:1-47)
Ammon (49:1-6)
Edom (49:7-22)
Damascus (49:23-27)
Kedar/Hazor (49:28-33)
Elam (49:34-49)
Babylon (50:1 to 51:64)

## Interpreting Life in Retrospect (52:1-34)

Chapter 52 reviews Judah's fate in retrospect. All the while it warns the reader of one's awesome fate for ignoring or rejecting the Word of the Lord through the prophet Jeremiah.

## Lessons for Life from Jeremiah 40—52

*Inability to learn from past mistakes closes the future to the achievement of life's purpose.*—People who remained in Judah following Jerusalem's fall repeated the same mistakes which had destroyed the nation. Today, only as persons incorporate their past misfortunes into a broader portrait of present action may their futures emerge with dynamic power.

*Ishmael's revolt against Gedaliah focuses on the imperative need to identify evil and to deal with it courageously and wisely when it first appears.*—Naive leaders who mistakenly evaluate malicious persons' motives do a disservice to God's larger purposes. The risks of adopting unethical standards in dealing with such issues is apparent; thereby, people may become as immoral as the evil they oppose. God's people must act without compromising their ethical stance.

*Jeremiah's oracles on the nations reaffirm for every generation that the nations of this world are the kingdoms of our Lord and his Christ.* Whatever the images and figures of speech we may use to describe the reality of God's presence in history, people today need to recapture an awareness of divine providence. Too often, we succumb to the belief that hostile powers have hijacked the world and now hold it hostage. Despite all evidences to the contrary, faith continues to insist: "This is my Father's world."[2]

---

1. Pauline Rush Evans, ed., *Book One: The Family Treasury of Children's Stories* (Garden City, N.Y.: Doubleday & Co., 1956), p. 33.
2. Words by Mattie D. Babcock.

# Personal Learning Activities

1. Following the fall of Jerusalem, the remnant would need
   _____ and _____ in order to renew the
   nation and its relationship to God. (Choose the correct answers from the list.)
   - (1) A new king
   - (2) A new temple
   - (3) New hearts
   - (4) New spirits
   - (5) Better prophets
   - (6) Rebuilt cities

2. Match the following two lists, linking the terms in the first
   column with the identifying phrases in the second column.
   - _____(1) Jeremiah
   - _____(2) Nebuzaradan
   - _____(3) Gedaliah
   - _____(4) Johanan
   - _____(5) Ishmael

   - (a) Freed Jeremiah
   - (b) Governor of the cities of Judah
   - (c) Killed the governor appointed by the Babylonians
   - (d) Taken in chains to Ramah
   - (e) Warned the governor that a plot existed to kill him

3. Under Johanan's leadership, the remnant fled into _____ .
   (Select the proper response from the list.)
   - (1) Edom
   - (2) Babylon
   - (3) Egypt
   - (4) Assyria

4. In the country to which the remnant fled, the people began
   to worship _____ again. (Choose the
   correct answer from the list.)
   - (1) Baal
   - (2) Yahweh
   - (3) The golden calf
   - (4) The queen of heaven

**Answers:**
1. (3), (4); 2. (1)d, (2)a, (3)b, (4)e, (5)c; 3. (3); 4. (4)

140

# THE CHURCH STUDY COURSE

The Church Study Course consists of a variety of short-term credit courses for adults and youth and noncredit foundational units for children and preschoolers. The materials are for use in addition to the study and training curriculums made available to the churches on an ongoing basis.

Study courses and foundational units are organized into a system that is promoted by the Sunday School Board, 127 Ninth Avenue, North, Nashville, Tennessee 37234; by the Woman's Missionary Union, 600 North Twentieth Street, Birmingham, Alabama 35203; by the Brotherhood Commission, 1548 Poplar Avenue, Memphis, Tennessee 38104; and by the respective departments of the state conventions affiliated with the Southern Baptist Convention.

Study course materials are flexible enough to be adapted to the needs of any Baptist church. The resources are published in several different formats—textbooks of various sizes, workbooks, and kits. Each item contains a brief explanation of the Church Study Course and information on requesting credit. Additional information and interpretation are available from the participating agencies.

### Types of Study and Credit

Adults and youth can earn study course credit through individual or group study. Teachers of courses or of foundational units are also eligible to receive credit.

1. Class Experience.—Group involvement with course material for the designated number of hours for the particular course. A person who is absent from one or more sessions must complete the "Personal Learning Activities" or other requirements for the course.
2. Individual Study.—This includes reading, viewing, or listening to course material and completing the specified requirements for the course.
3. Lesson Course Study.—Parallel use of designated study course material during the study of selected units in

Church Program Organization periodical curriculum units. Guidance for this means of credit appears in the selected periodical.
4. Institutional Study.—Parallel use of designated study course material during regular courses at educational institutions, including Seminary Extension Department courses. Guidance for this means of credit is provided by the teacher.

Credit is awarded for the successful completion of a course of study. This credit is granted by the Church Study Course Awards Office, 127 Ninth Avenue, North, Nashville, Tennessee 37234, for the participating agencies. Form 151 (available free) is recommended for use in requesting credit.

When credit is issued to a person on request, the Awards Office sends two copies of a notice of credit earned to the church. The original copy of the credit slip should be filed by the study course clerk in the participant's record of training folder. The duplicate should be given to the person who earned the credit. Accumulated credits are applied toward leadership or member development diplomas, which are measures of learning, growth, development, and training.

Detailed information about the Church Study Course system of credits, diplomas, and record keeping is available from the participating agencies. Study course materials, supplementary teaching or learning aids, and forms for record keeping may be ordered from Baptist Book Stores.

**The Church Study Course Curriculum**
Credit is granted on those courses listed in the current copy of *Church Services and Materials Catalog* and *Baptist Book Store Catalog*. When selecting courses or foundational units, check the current catalogs to determine what study course materials are valid.

**How to Request Credit for This Course**
This book is the text for a course in the subject area Bible Study.

This course is designed for 5 hours of group study. Credit is awarded for satisfactory class experience with the study material for the minimum number of hours. A person who is absent from one or more sessions must complete the "Personal Learning Activities" or other requirements for the materials missed.

Credit also is allowed for use of this material in individual study and in institutional study, if so designated.

The following requirements must be met for credit in this course:

1. Read the book *Jeremiah: Witness Under Pressure.*
2. Attend at least 5 hours of class study or complete all "Personal Learning Activities" (see end of each chapter). A class member who is absent from one or more class sessions must complete "Personal Learning Activities" on chapters missed. In such a case, he must turn in his paper by the date the teacher sets, usually within ten days following the last class.

Credit in this course may be earned through individual study. The requirements for such credit are:

1. Read the book.
2. Complete the "Personal Learning Activities" on the chapters.

Credit in this course may be earned through study in an educational institution, if so designated by a teacher. The requirements are:

1. Read the book.
2. Fulfill the requirements of the course taught at the institution.

After the course is completed, the teacher, the study course records librarian, the learner, or any person designated by the church should complete Form 151 ("Church Study Course Credit Request, Revised 1975") and send it to the Awards Office, 127 Ninth Avenue, North, Nashville, Tennessee 37234. In the back of this book the reader will find a form which he may cut out, fill in, and send to the Awards Office.

INSTRUCTIONS: If requested by the teacher, fill in this form and give it to him when the course is completed. If preferred, mail this request for course credit to

**AWARDS OFFICE**
**THE SUNDAY SCHOOL BOARD, SBC**
**127 NINTH AVENUE, NORTH**
**NASHVILLE, TENNESSEE 37234**

| State Convention | Association | Indicate Type of Study (X) |
|---|---|---|
| | | ☐ Class   ☐ Individual   ☐ Lesson Course   ☐ Educational Institution |

**CHURCH**

Church Name

Mailing Address

City, State, Zip Code

**MAIL TO**

Mail to (if Different from Church Address)

Street, Route, or P.O. Box

City, State, Zip Code

| LAST NAME | FIRST NAME AND MIDDLE INITIAL | MRS. (X) | COURSE TITLE |
|---|---|---|---|
| | | | |
| | | | |
| | | | |
| | | | |
| | | | |